Simple Solutions.
Minutes a Day-Mastery for a Lifetime!

Level 4
2nd Semester

English Grammar & Writing Mechanics

Nancy McGraw and Nancy Tondy

Bright Ideas Press, LLC
Cleveland, OH

Simple Solutions Level 4
English Grammar & Writing Mechanics

Printed in the United States of America

ISBN: 978-1-60873-072-8

Cover Design: Dan Mazzola
Editor: Kimberly A. Dambrogio
Randall L. Reetz

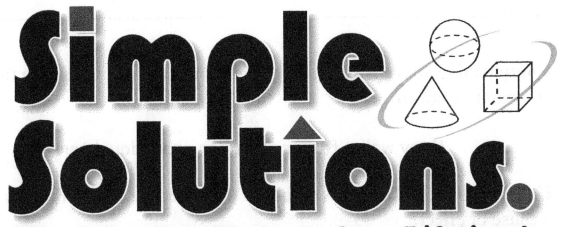

Welcome

Simple Solutions.
Minutes a Day-Mastery for a Lifetime!

Note to the Student:

We hope that this program will help you understand <u>English Grammar & Writing Mechanics</u> concepts better than ever. For many of you, it will help you to have a more positive attitude toward learning these skills.

Using this workbook will give you the opportunity to practice skills you have learned in previous grades. By practicing these skills each night, you will gain confidence in your reading, writing, and speaking ability.

In order for this program to help you, it is extremely important that you do a lesson every day. It is also important that you ask your teacher for help with the items that you don't understand or that you get wrong on your homework.

We hope that through Simple Solutions and hard work, you discover how satisfying and how much fun language can be!

Lesson #73

1. A suffix is added to the end of a word to change the meaning of the word. The suffix *–est* means "most" and the suffix *–er* means "more."
   Example: fastest → most fast, faster → more fast
   Write the words that mean "more slow" and "most slow."

   _____   _____

2. **Comparative adverbs compare two actions (verbs).** Underline the comparative adverb.

   Mary walks faster than her granddaughter!

3. **Cause** tells **why**; **effect** tells **what**. Is the underlined part of the sentence a <u>cause</u> or <u>effect</u>?

   <u>The temperature was 92°</u>, so Ethan was very uncomfortable.

   cause   effect

4. The exact, or literal meaning of a word is its _____.

   denotation   connotation

5. Write a plural subject pronoun to replace the underlined words.

   <u>Casey and Billy</u> are champion swimmers.   _____

6. Underline the singular possessive noun.

   Have you seen Norm's baseball cards?

7. Choose the correct contraction.

   Ray and Joe (isn't / aren't / ain't) coming to our practice.

8. Write the verb using future tense.

   Next we _____ _____ a history of the Hopewell Indians.
                           (study)

9. Write the irregular plurals.   calf   thief   half

   _____   _____   _____

10. Draw the editing mark that tells you to indent or begin a new paragraph.

    _____

11. A fragment is not a complete thought. Draw a line through the fragment.

    The Hopewell Indians were Mound Builders. Many beautiful artifacts. These artifacts teach us about the lifestyle of the Hopewell.

12. Look at the editing marks and rewrite the sentences correctly.

    The Hopewell Indians were great artists⊙ Archeologists have found ʃewelry and pottery made ˌthe Hopewell.
                                                      by

    _____

    _____

    _____

Lesson #74

1. Fill in a word to complete the analogy.

    throw : catch :: laugh :_____

    cry   giggle   scream

2. Match each suffix or prefix with its meaning. *pre-   -er   -less   -ful*

    more - _____   full of - _____

    without - _____   before - _____

3. <u>Nadia was disappointed</u> because her team lost the game.
    What does the underlined part of the sentence tell?

    cause   effect

4. Choose the word that has the most positive connotation.

    I like the (odor / scent / smell) of Enola's perfume.

5. _____ is the final step of The Writing Process.

6. Insert quotation marks.

    How many of you are there? asked the troll.

7. Choose the verb in each set that shows past tense.

    happen / happened   touched / touch   colored / color

8. Underline three adjectives.

   Grandpa gave me three brushes, green paint, and a large apron.

9. What pronoun is used as the object in the sentence above? _____

10. Choose the correct past tense verb.

    The girls had (drive / drove / driven) the go-cart on the sidewalk.

11. Use the editing mark for capitalization to show which proper nouns should be capitalized.

    I invited flora and david to come with us to disneyland.

12. Rewrite this sentence correctly.

    We will fly travel by plane to Florida⊙

    _____

    _____

Lesson #75

1. The suffix *–less* means "without." Use the suffix *–less* to write words that match the meanings below.

    without rest → _____

    without a name → _____

2. Tell what each suffix means.

    –less _____   *-est* _____   *-ful* _____

3. Underline the plural pronoun in each sentence.

    We brought Ben and Abe to school. Mom made their lunches. Ben carried them.

4. Look at the pronouns you chose in the item above. Write each pronoun next to its type.

    subject pronoun _____   object pronoun_____

    possessive pronoun _____

5. Choose a synonym for the underlined word.

    Valerie was <u>absent</u> from school on Monday because she had the flu.

    missing   late   early   present

6. Your little dog follows you everywhere. He is so <u>devoted</u> to you! The underlined word means _____.

    loyal   afraid   sleepy   smart

7. Nathan finished his homework <u>just</u> before dinner.
   What does the underlined word mean?

          fair   simply   shortly   wrong

8. Find the word *finale* in a dictionary and look at the pronunciation key.
   Which word rhymes with *finale*?

           sale   spinal   trolley

9. What is the meaning of *finale*?

         last   beginning   end   fish

10 – 12. What is your favorite day of the week? Write your day in the
   center of the circle and list the reasons why it is your favorite day
   in the spaces around it.

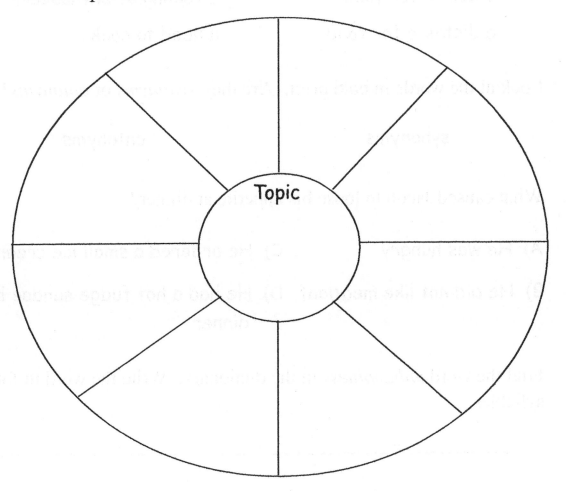

Lesson #76

Read the paragraph and use it to answer items 1 – 4.

Jacob poked his fork at his meatloaf, moving the food around his plate. He had no <u>appetite</u> at dinner. Normally he would have been hungry, but today he had eaten a **gigantic** hot fudge (sundae / Sunday) after school. Jacob (knew / new) that next time he would order a **small** ice cream cone.

1. Choose the correct homophone in each set of parentheses ( ).

2. What is the meaning of the underlined word in the paragraph?

      a desire for food   a feeling of enthusiasm

      a distaste for food   a need to cook

3. Look at the words in bold print. Are they *synonyms* or *antonyms*?

      synonyms   antonyms

4. What caused Jacob to loose his appetite at dinner?

    A) He was hungry.   C) He ordered a small ice cream cone

    B) He did not like meatloaf. D) He had a hot fudge sundae before dinner.

5. Find the word *unhappiness* in the dictionary. Write the word in four syllables.

_____ - _____ - _____ - _____

6. Correctly spell the plurals of these nouns. The first one has been done for you.   baby - <u>babies</u>

     daisy - _____ penny - _____ city - _____

7. Find the word *honest* in a thesaurus. Write two synonyms for *honest*.

_____   _____

8. Combine these sentences to make one sentence with a compound predicate.

Mrs. Kelly is Irish. Mrs. Kelly always celebrates St. Patrick's Day.

_____

_____

9. Underline each common noun in the sentence.

Mr. Cary plays tennis in the courts near our school.

10 – 12. Look at the graphic organizer you completed in Lesson #75. Use your notes to write an ad for your favorite day of the week.

_____

_____

_____

_____

Lesson #77

1. What is the root of all of these words?

    precooked, cooker, cooking, uncooked   _____

2 – 3. Study these homographs. Insert the letter of the word that should be
        used to complete each sentence.

    A) **desert** (di zúrt) v. to leave behind

    B) **desert** (dézzərt) n. area of land with little rain and vegetation

    If you talk in the theater I will _____ you at intermission!

    Our basement is as dry as a_____.

4. Some suffixes change a word from a verb to a noun. For example, the
    verb *act* becomes the noun *action* by adding –*ion*.
    Add -*ion* to these words.   elect   react   invent

    _____   _____   _____

5. Some other prefixes that mean "not" are *im*– and *il*–. For example,
    illegal means "not legal" and **im**possible means "not possible."
    Use these prefixes to reverse the meanings of these root words.

    polite ➜ im_____   logical ➜ il_____

6. Replace the underlined words with a contraction.

    Miguel <u>can not</u> stay after school today.   _____

7. Remember, irregular verbs do not end in –*ed*. Write the past tenses of
    run.

    _____, has/had/have _____

8. Use a comma to separate independent clauses in a compound sentence. Study the first sentence, and insert a comma in the second sentence.

We finished the snowman, and we went inside

for hot cocoa.   We enjoyed the cocoa but we

wanted to get started on our snow fort.

9. Which is incorrect?   Mr. bean   Johnny   Chicago

10. Combine these two sentences to make one sentence with a compound predicate.

June plays soccer. June enjoys watching movies.

_____

_____

11 – 12. Rewrite this run-on.

The biggest snow storm of the year came on my birthday
so no one could go out so I had to postpone my party!

_____

_____

_____

Lesson #78

1. What is the root of these words? _____

    employer   unemployed   employee   employment

2. Choose the word with the best connotation for this sentence.

    Nila likes her chili very (hot / burning / warm).

3. Alexis was growing fast, so <u>she needed new shoes every few months</u>. What does the underlined part of the sentence tell?

    cause   effect

4. Underline the adverb that tells *when*.

    We sometimes celebrate Valentine's Day with a party.

5. Choose the correct verb form in this sentence.

    I will (pour, pours) the soda into a glass.

6. Underline the verb that shows *being* in the sentence.

    I am an excellent baseball player.

7. Capitalize words that name family members only when they <u>name</u> the person. **Example**: my cousin, Cousin Carol
   Underline the family members that are written correctly.

    your mom   your Mom   uncle Henry   Uncle Henry

8. In an analogy, one word may name a part of the other.
    Example: wheels : bicycle :: legs : table
                  A *bicycle* has *wheels*. A *table* has *legs*.
    Fill in a word to complete the analogy.

    leaf : tree :: petal : _____

    stem   flower   leaf

9. Add a possessive noun to complete the sentence.

    _____ class is in the media center.
    (Mrs. Nixon)

10. Choose the helping verb that agrees with the subject.

    Tony and Zoe (has / have) carried the suitcases upstairs.

11. The <u>lead</u> in old paint is dangerous. In this sentence, *lead* means.

    old paint   a heavy metal   front of the line

12. Look at the underlined word in number 11.
    Does it rhyme with *said* or *seed*?

    said   seed

Lesson #79

1. Which word shows *being* in this sentence?

    I am the first in line.

2. Replace the underlined words with a contraction. _____

    The boxes <u>would not</u> fit in
    the trunk of the car.

3. **The puppies were <u>lovable</u>.** Choose a synonym for *lovable*.

    excited   noisy   messy   adorable

4. Match the meaning with the correct spelling.

    opposite of yes - _____ (no / know)

5. Underline the subject pronoun.   We are thirsty!

6. Is the pronoun in item 5 singular or plural? _____

7. What is the root of these words?

    useful   useless   misuse   usable   _____

8. Insert quotation marks and commas.

    Billy asked Where is Suzie?
    It's not my day to watch her replied Carla.

9. Use the editing marks for "check spelling" and "add something" to correct this sentence.

    We looked everywhere for Suzie but was nowhere to be fond.

10. Rewrite the sentence correctly.

    _____

    _____

11. Use the editing marks for "lower case" and "punctuation" to fix this sentence.

    Suzie was hiding under my Grandma's comforter

12. Rewrite the sentence correctly.

    _____

    _____

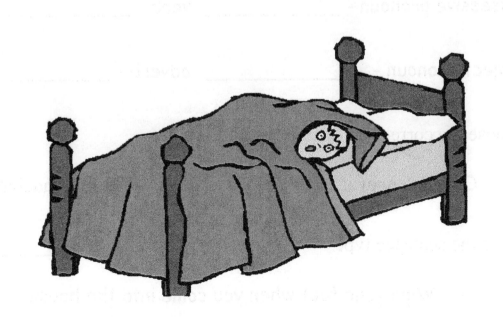

Lesson #80

Use this paragraph for items 1 through 4.

The Shawnee Indian, <u>Tecumseh</u>, was considered a powerful warrior. Tecumseh's name meant "panther lying in wait." He was born in <u>the</u> area now known as western Ohio, and he <u>fought</u> <u>fearlessly</u> for the rights of his <u>people</u> to keep their land and continue their culture. Tecumseh and his brother, The Prophet, were killed by American settlers in the early 1800's. <u>They</u> are remembered as <u>brave</u> leaders who wanted to unite Native Americans and preserve <u>their</u> way of life.

Facts taken from www.u-s-history.com.

Read the paragraph and look at how the underlined words are used. Write each underlined word next to its part of speech.

1. plural noun - _____ article - _____

2. proper noun - _____ adjective - _____

3. possessive pronoun - _____ verb - _____

4. subject pronoun - _____ adverb - _____

5. Choose the correct spelling of the adverb.

   Orville (careful / carefully) built wings for the machine.

6. Name the sentence type. _____

   Wipe your feet when you come into the house.

7.   A root word has no prefix or suffix. What is the root of all these words?

premix   mixer   mixed   remix   unmixed

_____

8.   Prefixes change the meaning of a root word. The prefix *un–* means
     "not." Add *un–* to make the opposite of the root word.
     Example: clear ➜ unclear

button ➜ _____   even ➜ _____

9.   Suffixes are word endings that change the meaning of a word. Match
     these suffixes with their meanings.   –er   –est   –ful   –less

without - _____   more - _____   full of - _____   most - _____

10. What is the denotation (literal meaning) of the underlined word?
          Use laundry bleach to remove <u>stubborn</u> stains.

pig-headed   willful   hard to get out

11. Use the editing marks for "take out something" and "check spelling" to
     correct this sentence.

          Flora wants to spend some time in at the beech.

12. Rewrite the sentence correctly.

_____

_____

Lesson #81

1. The Greek word *bios* means "life." When you see a word with *bio* in it, the word probably has something to do with "life." Match these words with their meanings.

    biology   the story of someone's life

    biography   the study of life

2. Write **past**, **present**, or **future** to tell the tense of these verbs.

    planned _____   invites _____   will ask _____

3. Use the words in the box to make compound words to complete the sentence.

fall	time	lunch	rain	water	bow

    At _____ (meal + noon) we saw a

    _____ (colors in the sky) over the

    _____ (river going over a cliff).

4. Check the spelling of these words. Cross out a misspelled word and write it correctly below.

    genaral   discover   confusion

    _____

5. Add the plural of *penny*.

    Nick had two dimes, three

    nickels and six_____.

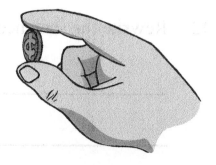

6. Fill in a word to complete the analogy.

    child : family :: student : _____

          teacher   class   book

7. Fill in an article to complete the sentence.

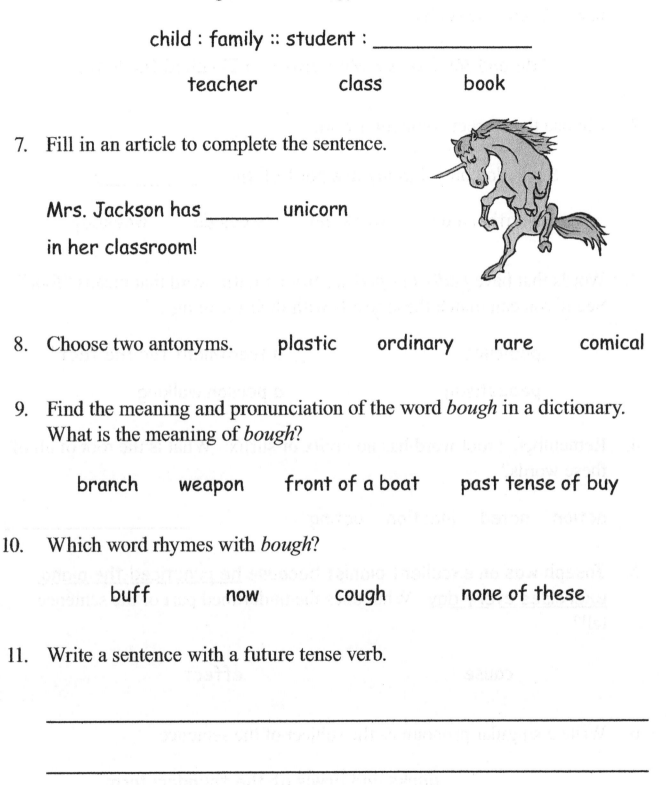

    Mrs. Jackson has _____ unicorn

    in her classroom!

8. Choose two antonyms.   plastic   ordinary   rare   comical

9. Find the meaning and pronunciation of the word *bough* in a dictionary.
    What is the meaning of *bough*?

        branch   weapon   front of a boat   past tense of buy

10. Which word rhymes with *bough*?

        buff   now   cough   none of these

11. Write a sentence with a future tense verb.

    _____

    _____

12. Underline the subject of your sentence in item 11.

Lesson #82

1. **When you write about another person and yourself, list your self last.** Choose the subject.

   (Me and Mr. Lewis / Mr. Lewis and I) raked the leaves.

2. Choose the correct compound word.

   Saturday and Sunday are part of the _____.

   weatherman   weekend   wayside   weekday

3. Words that have *pedi–* or *–ped* are from a Latin word that means "foot." See if you can match these words with their meanings.

   pedicure   a treatment for the feet

   pedestrian   a person walking

4. Remember, a root word has no prefix or suffix. What is the root of all of these words?

   action   acted   inaction   acting   _____

5. Joseph was an excellent pianist because <u>he practiced the piano exercises every day</u>. What does the underlined part of the sentence tell?

   cause   effect

6. Write a singular pronoun as the subject of the sentence.

   _____ barks and howls at the thunderstorm.

7. **Use a comma before or after a quote.**
   Example: Laura exclaimed, "What a beautiful song!" or
                  "Let's get some ice cream," said Jack.
   Do not use a comma at the end of the quote if there is another punctuation mark.
   Example: "Grandma's here!" exclaimed Sasha.
   Insert commas where they are needed.

   Liza asked "Can we go to the toy store?"

   "I doubt that we will have time for that " said Mom.

   "I never get to do any shopping!" complained Liza.

8. This sentence has a <u>helping verb</u> and a <u>main verb</u>. Underline the helping verb.

   I am working indoors today.

9. <u>She had</u> gone to the post office before school.
   Write a contraction to replace the underlined words.   _____

10. Underline the possessive pronoun.

    When the door slammed, both cats ran into their beds.

11. Write the plural form of each noun.   wolf - _____

    trouble - _____ city - _____

12. Write this sentence correctly.

    Next year i will go to summer camp with my friends

    _____

Lesson #83

1. Write the verb in the past tense.

    The monkeys _____ to the top of the tree.
                        (climb)

2. Find the plural subject pronoun and put a line under it.

    We have many things to do before the trip.

3. Write the words that were used to form the contraction.

    I was sure I'd never been to Atlanta before.   _____

4. Underline the possessive pronoun in this sentence.

    The duckling followed its mother all day.

5. Underline an objective case pronoun in the predicate of this sentence.

    Aliza picked fresh flowers and gave them to Mrs. Marx.

6. The words *credit*, *credible*, and *creed* all come from a Latin word
    meaning "to believe." Which word means "believable"?

    credit   credible   creed

7. Choose the word with the most positive connotation.

    Aimee's puppy is very

    (scrawny / undersized / tiny).

8. The suffix *–er* can also mean "someone who does something."
   Example: A teach<u>er</u> is <u>one who teaches</u>.
   Write the word that means "one who paints."

   _____

9. Sometimes the spelling of the root word changes when you add *–ion*,
   –sion, or *–tion*. Look at the examples, and then form the new words.
   Use a dictionary to check your work.
   Example: locate + -ion ➜ location, divide + -sion ➜ division

   create + -ion ➜ _____ decide + -sion ➜ _____

Look in a thesaurus or dictionary to find a more interesting word to
replace each word that is underlined. Write the words below.

Last summer we grew <u>pretty</u> flowers and <u>tasty</u> vegetables
                          10.   11.

in our garden. We learned how to <u>till</u> soil and plant seeds.
                                  12.

10. _____

11. _____

12. _____

Lesson #84

Read the paragraph and look at the underlined parts. If there is a mistake choose the correction. If there is no mistake choose "no error."

Two very famous brothers were <u>wilbur and orville</u>
                                                          1.

Wright. <u>The brothers was</u> very close friends, who often
                        2.

<u>made their own toys</u> and played together for hours. When
          3.

they grew up they built the very <u>first airplain</u>.
                                                    4.

1. Wilbur and orville
    Wilbur and Orville
    wilbur and orville
    no error

3. maked their own toys
    made they own toys
    made there own toys
    no error

2. The brothers' was
    the brothers were
    The brothers were
    no error

4. First Airplane.
    first airplane.
    first aeroplane.
    no error

5. List any two common nouns from the paragraph above.

_____   _____

6. Choose **two** synonyms for the word in bold print.

    home: dwelling   sea   habitat   wasteland

7. Underline the word that rhymes with the *bass* that is pictured.

place   class   lace   moss

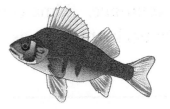

8. Look at the underlined words and match each word with its meaning.

The <u>authorship</u> of that <u>ancient</u> work is <u>anonymous</u>.
      A)   B)   C)

_____ an unknown person   _____ very old

_____ creator / origin of written work

9. Rewrite these to make one sentence with a compound predicate.

Dora is ten years old. Dora is in the fourth grade.

_____

10. Choose **two** synonyms for the word in bold print.

discover: read   find   uncover   hear

11. Make a contraction from the two underlined words in the sentence.

I <u>have not</u> ever seen an elephant.   _____

12. Write this sentence correctly.

The Wright Brothers were born in near Dayton, Ohio.

_____

_____

Lesson #85

1. **A preposition is a word that ties a noun or pronoun to other words in a sentence.** Some common prepositions are listed in the *Help Pages* in the back of this book. Find the list and write three prepositions here.

    _____   _____   _____

2. The word *photo* is from a Greek word meaning "light." Match each word with its meaning.

    photosynthesis   to print an image with light

    photograph   using light energy from the sun to make food

3. Fill in a word to complete the analogy.

    baseball : sport :: saxophone : _____

    flute   instrument   music

4. Does the underlined part of the sentence tell a *cause* or an *effect*?

    Boyd and Dacey were excited when <u>they received an</u>
    <u>invitation to the birthday party!</u>

    cause   effect

5. Choose the word with the most favorable connotation.

    Mrs. Dowd's puppy is very (unruly / active / wild).

6. Insert a comma where one is needed.

    Andrew asked "Does anyone want to play a board game?"

7. Underline the adverb that tells where.

Danny looked everywhere for his camera.

8. Fill in the plural subject pronoun in the second sentence.

Rene and Kim play pool games. _____ laugh and play all day.

9. Choose the correct verb form in this sentence.

They (carry / carries) boxes from the basement.

10 – 12. **Prewriting**   Name a food you like to eat. List some words to describe the food.

_____

_____

_____

_____

Lesson #86

1. A preposition shows the relationship between words in a sentence. List three additional prepositions from the *Help Pages*.

    _____   _____   _____

2. What is the root of these words?

    unclear   clearly   clearer   cleared   _____

3. Here are three more prefixes that mean "not": *in–, ir–, dis–*. Match each word with its meaning.

    invalid   not responsible

    irresponsible   not showing respect

    disrespect   not valid

4. Add quotation marks.

    Who will be coming to your party? asked Olivia.

    I hope you know you're invited, replied Emma.

5. Underline all the adjectives in this sentence.

    On a cold and dreary night nothing tastes
    better than a hot cup of chocolate milk.

6. Insert an object pronoun to complete the sentence.

    The director gave Donna a costume and she wore _____.

7. Choose the pronoun that agrees with the subject.

    Peter will sail (him / his) ship tomorrow.

8. Rewrite this sentence correctly.

    Amelia Earhart was a famous ~~W~~oman a~~nd~~ pilot.

    _____

9. What is missing in this fragment?

    My mother's red car.

    a subject   a verb

10 – 12. **Rough Draft**   Write three or four sentences describing a food you
          enjoy.

    _____

    _____

    _____

    _____

    _____

Lesson #87

1. List three more prepositions from the *Help Pages*. Do not repeat any prepositions that you listed in Lessons #85 or #86.

   _____   _____   _____

2. What is the denotation of a word?

        the exact meaning   the feeling connected with a word

3. Choose the correct future tense verb.

       The postal carrier (will come / had come) before noon.

4. Underline the helping verb.

   Anthony might run in

   the race tomorrow.

5. Insert a possessive noun.

   Lori got a new board game for her birthday. We will probably play

   with _____ new game at recess.

6. Underline the nouns that are singular.

       Look in your desk for some markers, a tablet, and an eraser.

7. Write the plural form of each noun.   peach   wolf   child

   _____   _____   _____

8. Always begin a sentence with a _____.

9. The <u>shallow</u> water barely covered my ankles. What does *shallow* mean?

    deep   muddy   low   cold

10. Find the word *gander* in the dictionary and write its meaning on the line.

    _____

11. Read this sentence carefully. What is wrong with it?

    Phillis Wheatley was a gifted child even though she had been kidnapped from Africa and sold into slavery she learned to speak English and not only that she became an excellent poet but she died young.

    _____

12. Rewrite this sentence correctly.

    Phillis learned to read the (hole) Bible in less ʌtwo years.
                                      sp   than

    _____

    _____

Lesson #88

1. Underline the prepositions. Use the *Help Pages* to check your work.

   above walks below several inside people during lightly

2. Choose the correct verb form in the sentence.

   I (am / are) in Mrs. Green's fourth grade class.

3. Form the past tense of the verb to complete this sentence.

   Sierra _____ three and two to get the product.
   (multiply)

4. Underline the plural nouns.

   The girls had sandwiches, milk, and cookies for lunch.

5. Underline the proper nouns.

   Charles Brush invented electric lighting
   and Thomas Edison improved it.

6. Draw a line under the subject of this sentence.

   Brush's invention allowed people to go out at
   night on lighted city streets and sidewalks.

7. Choose the correct homophone.

   We will eat lunch in about an (hour / our).

8. Check the spelling of these plurals. Cross out any that are misspelled and write them correctly on the line.

shelfs   oxen   pigeons   locks   womans

_____

9. Look in a dictionary or thesaurus and find a better word to replace the underlined word. Write your word below.

Charles Brush became <u>rich</u> and was very generous to people in need.

_____

10. Revise this sentence. Rewrite it so that the sentence makes more sense.

The study of science was important to Charles donated money.

_____

_____

11. Combine these sentences. Write one sentence with a compound subject.

Charles Brush made electric lighting possible. Thomas Edison made electric lighting possible.

_____

_____

12. Insert the editing marks for "lower case" and "punctuation" to fix this sentence.

Today we can't imagine life without Electricity

Lesson #89

1. A preposition shows the relationship between words in a sentence.
   Example: Timmy hiked <u>through</u> the Grand Canyon.
   Underline the preposition.

   He walked beside his sister.

2. **A prepositional phrase is made up of a preposition followed by a noun or pronoun.** What is the preposition in each prepositional phrase?

   Kayla ate popcorn <u>during the movie</u>.   _____

   She shared the popcorn <u>with Devin</u>.   _____

3. Write the present tense form of *smile* in this sentence.

   Melissa is always _____ at Charlie.

4. Choose the correct homophone.

   Benny is always running (here / hear) and there!

5. Choose an antonym for the underlined word.

   As the sun comes up the temperature will <u>rise</u>.

   soar   climb   maintain   fall

6. Replace the underlined words with a contraction.

   Marla and Jim wondered if <u>they had</u> been late.   _____

7. Look in a dictionary. What is the meaning of *legible*?

   _____

8.   These are the prefixes that mean "not": *un–*, *im–*, *il–*, *dis–*, *in–*, *ir–*. Use
     these prefixes to make words mean the opposite of their roots.
     Example: in- + correct → incorrect (not correct)
     Use *il–* to write a word that means the opposite of *legible*.

     _____

9 – 12.   Here is a writing sample that has been
          revised. Rewrite the paragraph correctly.

Street lighting ʌCharles Brush created the electric arc
          began when
light. Brush's invention made it safe for people to go ʌin
                                                        travel
Cleveland's Public Square after dark. People began going out
                                              ʌ
                                             so they
more at night. People were able to work. In other places too.
                                            ʌ
                                         late at night
Soon, ʌcities like San Francisco and New York began using
      other
Brush's invention. They used it to light their streets and

roads at night.

     _____

     _____

     _____

     _____

Lesson #90

Read the paragraph and use it to complete the first six items.

       Tristan was nervous about his visit to an <u>ophthalmologist</u>. He had never had his eyes examined by a doctor, but lately he was having trouble seeing the words on the board in his classroom. The ophthalmologist smiled at Tristan and told him the exam wouldn't hurt a bit. She used a special light to look at Tristan's **cornea**. Then she asked him to read letters that were projected onto the wall. Finally, the ophthalmologist prescribed corrective lenses. Tristan was relieved and happy because he could see so (clear / clearly) with his new glasses.

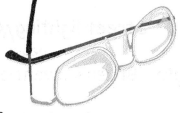

1. Underline the correct word to complete the last sentence of the paragraph.

2. What is the meaning of the underlined word?

       a nervous condition   a type of glasses

       an eye doctor   none of these

3. What is the meaning of the word *cornea*?

       part of the eye   a special light

       a place where two walls meet   a doctor

4. Which of these states a *cause*?

    <u>Tristan was having trouble seeing</u>, so <u>he had his eyes examined</u>.
              A   B

5. Which of these states an *effect*?

    <u>Tristan was happy and relieved</u>, because <u>he could see clearly</u>.
              A   B

6. Underline two synonyms: **eyeglasses   worried   cornea   nervous**

7. Look at the prepositional phrase that is underlined. Find the preposition and write it on the line.

    We looked for footprints <u>along the path</u>.

    _____

8. Make nouns by adding the suffix *–sion* to these verbs: explode, confuse. Use a dictionary to check your work.

    _____   _____

9. Choose the word with the most positive connotation.

    We were given a (skimpy / meager / light) lunch.

10. Fill in a singular subject pronoun.

    Edward likes to hike. _____ hikes through the parks all day.

11. Choose the correct past tense verb.

    My sisters have (draw / drew / drawn) the letters on the poster.

12. Insert commas where they belong.

    Should I get a yellow umbrella a pair of gloves a rain hat or a tote bag?

Lesson #91

1. Ben knew <u>he had</u> forgotten his glove. Write a contraction to replace the underlined words.

   _____

2. Find the preposition in the prepositional phrase and write it on the line

   Lucy lives in the apartment <u>behind our house</u>.

   _____

3. Fill in a word to complete the analogy.

   second : minute :: minute : _____

   hour   time   day

4. Words containing *graph* come from a Greek word that means "write." Use what you know about other origins to match these words with their meanings.

   a section of writing   autograph

   written in one's own hand   graphite

   material used for writing   paragraph

5. Place a ✓ next to the prefixes that mean "not."

   ____ un-   ____ re-   ____ dis-   ____ im-   ____ in-

   ____ ir-   ____ pre-   ____ il-   ____ mis-

6. Which objective case pronoun can replace the underlined words?

   "Will you take <u>my sister and me</u> with you?" pleaded Marie.

   _____

7 – 8. Add quotation marks.

What will you do during spring break? asked Marie.

Carla answered right away. We're going to Florida to see my grandpa!

9 – 12. Narrow your topic by using an inverted triangle. Go from broad to narrow.

Example:

Complete the graphic organizer for writing about someone famous. Use these words:

Harriet Beecher Stowe   famous women

famous people   famous women writers

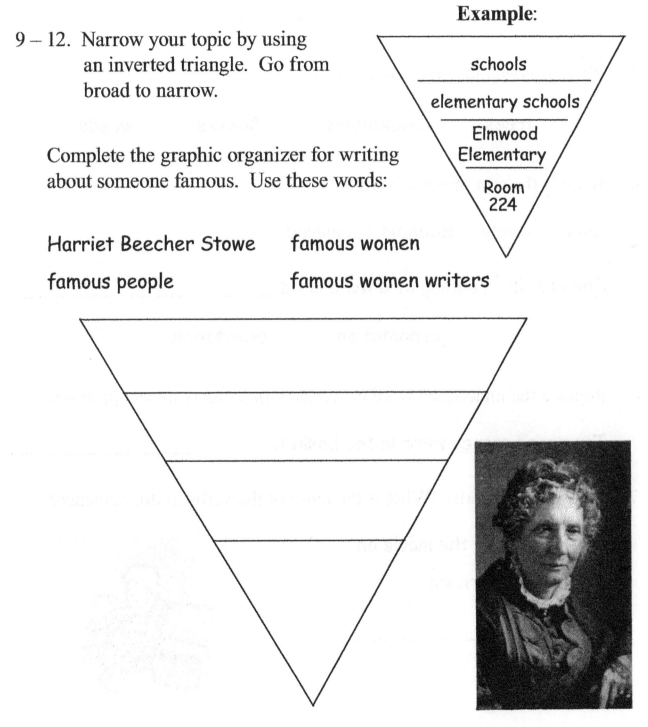

Lesson #92

1. Underline the prepositional phrase in this sentence.

   Let's plant some colorful petunias and impatiens around the tree.

2. Write the preposition from item 1 on the line.

   _____

3. What are *petunias* and *impatiens*?

   trees   vegetables   flowers   weeds

4. What is the root of these words?

   loved   lovely   loveable   unloved   _____

5. The specific meaning of a word is its _____.

   connotation   denotation

6. Replace the underlined word or words with a plural subject pronoun.

   <u>Ten paper cranes</u> were in the basket.   _____

7. Underline the verbs. What is the tense of the verbs in this sentence?

   Kaitlyn will see the movie on
   Saturday afternoon.

   _____

8. Underline the main verb in this sentence. Circle the helping verb.

    The lion cubs had grown too big for their cage.

9. Underline the plural possessive noun.

    Three men lifted the lions' cage and moved it.

Read the following paragraph, then answer the questions below.

    We cannot have a puppy because we live in an apartment.

    Our Apartment doesn't allow pets Maybe i can get one of

    those are electronic NeoPets.

10. Use the editing marks for "capital letter" and "take out" to make
    corrections to one of the sentences above.

11. Use the editing marks for "lower case" and "punctuation" to make two
    corrections in another sentence.

12. Underline the sentence that has no errors.

Lesson #93

1. Add prepositions to complete the sentence.

   Trevor ran _____ the street and _____ the tunnel.

2. Should you use the preposition *between* or *among*? Use *between* when speaking or writing about just two items.
   Example: The captain had to choose <u>between</u> Ethan and Jacob.
   Choose the best word to complete this sentence.

   I had a choice (between / among) a movie and roller skating.

3. **An abbreviation is a shortened form of a word.**
   Example: Mr.   Mrs.   U.S.A.   M.D.
   Titles that appear before a proper noun are capitalized and end in a period (except "Miss" and "Master"). Write the titles correctly.

   mr stewart   dr evans   miss demarco

   _____   _____   _____

4. Find the word *ruse* in a dictionary. What rhymes with *ruse*?

   rush   lose   bus   none of these

5. Write another word that means the same or almost the same as *ruse*.

   _____

6. Choose the correct homophone.

   Mom covered the broken window with a (bored / board).

7.　Choose an antonym for the underlined word.

Julian will <u>purchase</u> some tomatoes for canning.

discard　　　　　answer　　　　　buy　　　　　sell

8.　Rewrite the underlined words as a contraction.

Jason <u>will not</u> be in your class.　　　　　_____

9.　Fill in a word to complete the analogy.

rake : tool :: Florida : _____

south　　　　　city　　　　　state

10.　Choose the meaning of the underlined word.

Patty was sick all weekend and she is still feeling a little <u>feeble</u>.

better　　　　weak　　　　strong　　　　tough

11.　Underline the sentence that has no errors.

Armstrong was the furst man who ever walked on moon. Only a dozen people have ever walked on the moon.

12.　Use the editing marks for "check spelling" and "add something" to correct the other sentence in item 11.

Lesson #94

1. Underline the prepositional phrase.

   Let's sleep inside the tent!

2. The words *between* and *among* are prepositions. **Use *between* when
   speaking or writing about two nouns. Use *among* when speaking
   or writing about more than two. Examples:** Paul had to choose
   between a skating party and a sleepover.   Helen had to choose
   among lemon, strawberry, and butterscotch.

   Choose the correct preposition.

   I chose (between / among) Hector, Louis, and Orlando for
   team captain.

3. **For verbs that end in *–e*: Drop the *–e* when you add *–ed* to form the
   past tense of a verb. Example:** wiggle + -ed ➜ wiggled
   Form the past tense of the verb to complete this sentence.

   Dakota _____to get out of the rain.
            (race)

4. Write the titles correctly.

   miss waters   ms lerner   master Jacobs

   _____   _____   _____

5. Kwame is an excellent baker. He knows how to read a recipe and
   measure ingredients carefully. Mom thinks his brownies are the
   best!

   Underline the common nouns in the sentences above.

6. Place an editing mark that means "indent" in front of the first sentence in item 5.

7. List the proper nouns and pronouns that you see in the sentences in item 5.

    proper nouns – _____   _____

    pronouns – _____   _____

8 – 12. **Prewriting**   Think about why exercise is important to someone your age. What are some things you do for exercise? How can you get more exercise? Put your ideas in the boxes and complete the graphic organizer.

Lesson #95

1. You can remember that *between* is used for two items this way. *Between* has a *tw* just like the word *two*. Use *among* for more than two. Choose the correct preposition.

    We divided the work (between / among) the two of us.

    We shared the fudge (between / among) the three of us.

2. Underline the prepositional phrase.

    Fluffy buried her bone under the bushes.

3. **Social titles are abbreviated only when they appear before names.** Which is correct?

    Just where do you think you are you going, Mr.?

    Just where do you think you are you going, Mister?

4. Make these nouns plural.

    hoof   louse   sheep

    _____   _____   _____

5. Replace the underlined word or words with a plural subject pronoun.

    <u>Carson and I</u> were mowing

    the lawn.

    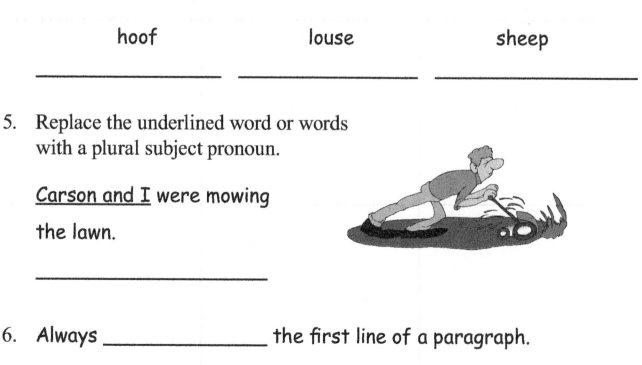

    _____

6. Always _____ the first line of a paragraph.

7. Find and underline two prepositions in this sentence.

Thomas hid behind the oak tree and

Maddie hid under the picnic table.

8 – 12. The second step of **The Writing Process** is
         writing a rough draft. Look at the graphic
         organizer you completed in the last lesson.
         Use your ideas to write a draft of at least five
         sentences.

_____

_____

_____

_____

_____

_____

_____

Lesson #96

1. Which is the correct preposition?

   Decide (between / among) the three of you, who will go first.

2. Underline the prepositional phrase.

   We love to hear music throughout the house.

3. Each state in the United States has a postal abbreviation.

   Notice that the postal abbreviation does not use a period. Do not use abbreviations in standard writing.

State	Postal
Ohio	OH
Virginia	VA
Kentucky	KY

   Instead, you should write the full name of a city, state, or country. Which is correct?

   Nick moved to Del. to live near his family.

   Nick moved to Delaware to live near his family.

4. Choose the correct verb form in this sentence.

   You (float / floats) the paper boat on the water.

5. Replace the underlined words with a contraction. _____

   Did you see what they have planted in the garden?

6. Choose the correct homophone.

   A (hair / hare) is bigger than a rabbit.

7. Write an antonym for each word by adding the prefix *dis–*.
    Example: obey ➜ disobey

    _____ (like) _____ (trust) _____ (agree)

8. Make nouns by adding the suffix *–ion* to these verbs: **instruct   deduct**
    Use a dictionary to check your work.

    _____   _____

9. Use a thesaurus to write three synonyms for the word *home*.

    _____ _____ _____

10. Choose the correct verb form.

    They (make, makes) castles in the sand.

11. Write a compound word that
    means "the light of day."

    _____

12. Combine these sentences and write one sentence with a compound
    predicate.

    Neil Armstrong was commander of Apollo 11. Neil Armstrong was
    the first man to walk on the moon.

    _____

    _____

Lesson #97

1. **Conjunctions connect words, phrases, or parts of a sentence.** Some common conjunctions are: *and, or, but,* and *so.* Write this list of conjunctions below.

    _____

2. **Use capital letters to abbreviate the words for temperature because these abbreviations come from proper nouns.**

    Example: °F ➡ degrees Fahrenheit, °C ➡ degrees Celsius.
                 The temperature today is -12°C, so bundle up!
    Write the abbreviated temperature correctly.

    ten degrees Fahrenheit   _____

3. In an analogy, the word may describe the other.
    Example: bright : sunshine :: prickly : porcupine
                 Sunshine is bright. A porcupine is prickly.
    Fill in a word to complete the analogy.

    light : feather ::_____ : sugar

    candy   sweet   cake

4. Underline the *cause* in this statement.

    There was a cold advisory, so school was cancelled today.

5. Choose the word with the best connotation for this sentence.

    Maybe you can go to the zoo with us. Why don't you (beg / ask / implore) your mother?

6. Underline the adverb that tells *where*.

    Let's go downtown for the holiday parade!

7. Add quotation marks correctly.

Mom, can I go to the zoo with Jasmine?

Did you finish your homework?

8. **Use a comma between two adjectives if they describe a noun in the same way or if you could use the word *and* between them.** The comma takes the place of the word *and*.
Example: Our soft, furry kittens are so much fun! You could write "Our furry, soft kittens..." or "Our soft *and* furry kittens..."
Insert a comma where it is needed.

I'm wearing my warm fuzzy slippers.

9. Underline all the adjectives in this sentence.

I used red, green, blue, and yellow balloons for a cheerful effect.

10. Choose the correct verb form to complete the sentence.

We always use that sweeper since it (clean / cleans) the carpet pretty well.

11. Choose the correct past tense verb.

Our dog has (ride / rode / ridden) in the baby's car seat!

12. Underline the sentence that has no errors. What is wrong with the other sentence?

We walked up and down the streets, searching for that dog.
In people's back yards! _____

Lesson #98

1. Underline the conjunction that joins two phrases in this sentence.

    Paulette wants a new bike but hasn't saved enough money
    to buy one.

2. Each day of the week has an abbreviation. Write each abbreviation next
    to its full name.   Wed .   Mon.   Sat.

    Monday _____ Wednesday _____ Saturday _____

3. Use *among* when there are three or more.
    Example: Mom divided the candy *among* Natalie, Seth, and Ashley.

    Choose the best word to complete this sentence.

    You can choose (between / among) strawberry, lemon, and
    watermelon.

4. Words that contain *auto* come from a Greek word that means "self." Use
    what you know to match these words with their meanings.

    autobiography   self-starting

    autograph   written by oneself

    automatic   the written story of one's own life

5. Make nouns by adding the suffix *–ion* to these verbs.   select   inject
    Use a dictionary to check your work.

    _____   _____

6. Find the subject pronoun.

    He may not be home since it is about time for his daily walk.

7. What is the root of these words?

      incorrect   correctly   corrected   incorrectly

       _____

8. Replace the underlined words with a plural subject pronoun.

<u>Those monkeys</u> are so wild and funny!

      _____

9. Add a helping verb and a future tense verb.

Later we _____ _____ our lunch together.

10. Fix this sentence with editing marks for "capitalization" and "check spelling."

    On friday we will perform our anual spring concert.

11. Rewrite the sentence in item 10 correctly.

    _____

    _____

12. Use an editing mark to fix a slight problem in this sentence.

    Mr Gee brought the sheet music for our practice.

Lesson #99

1. Should you use *good* or *well* to describe something? **The word *good* is an adjective; adjectives describe nouns.**
   Example: Trina makes *good* cookies!
   The word *well* is an adverb; adverbs describe verbs.
   Example: Angie played the flute *well* !
   Choose the correct word.

   You behaved (good / well) in the restaurant.

   You did a (good / well) job on your homework.

2. Notice in this example that there are two **main (independent) clauses.**
   Example: <u>Horace is fourteen now</u>, so <u>he can ride his bike to the park alone</u>. Each clause could be a sentence by itself. The clauses are joined by the conjunction *so* and there is a comma before the conjunction.
   Insert a comma and underline the conjunction in this sentence.

   Where are we going and how do we get there?

3. If you lose the game, don't <u>sulk</u>. You can try again next time.
   Someone who is *sulking* is:

   in a bad mood   feeling better   trying hard   winning

4. Write the abbreviations for *Monday* and *Wednesday*.

   _____   _____

5. Choose the best word to complete the sentence.

   You can choose (between / among) these three books for your

   book report.

6. In the phrase "use your head," the word *head* _____ brainpower.

   denotes   connotes

7. In the phrase "put a hat on your head," the word *head* _____ the part of the body which includes the skull.

    denotes   connotes

8. Underline the object pronoun.

    We forgot to give him directions.

9. Add a helping verb and the present tense verb to complete the sentence.

    People _____ _____ so loudly that I can barely hear you.
                  (cheer)

10. You know that you should use commas to separate items in a series. A sentence may have a **series of phrases**; a comma comes between each phrase. **Example**: Today I will go to the store, clean my room, and do some reading.

    Insert commas between the phrases.

    Bernice walked into the room looked at the puppies and

    began to laugh.

11. Choose the correct past tense verb.

    Mr. McAlister has already (shake / shook / shaken) the paint can.

12. Write this sentence correctly.

    Sunday it was the first day of Spring training, and we met our

    softball coach.

    _____

    _____

Lesson #100

Read the paragraph and look at the numbered items. If there is a mistake choose the correction. If the underlined item is correct choose "no error."

The music students walked onto the stage and <u>quiet took</u>
                                                                                  1.

<u>their seats</u>. Each of the students was dressed in black and carried
        2.

a wind instrument. They lifted their instruments to <u>they</u> lips and
                                                                              3.

began to tune. Then they were silent again. The conductor walked

onto the stage, bowed to <u>the audience</u> faced the students, and
                                                4.

raised his baton. A jazzy melody filled the <u>concert Hall</u> as the
                                                                    5.

<u>conductor's</u> hands and arms performed a frenzied dance.
        6.

1. quietly took	3. they're	5. Concert Hall
quite took	their	concert hall
no error	no error	no error
2. their seat	4. the audience,	6. conductors'
there seats	the Audience	conductors
no error	no error	no error

7. Find the meaning and pronunciation of the word *sieve* in a dictionary.
    Which word rhymes with *sieve*?

        give   hive   leave

8. Choose two synonyms for *sieve*.

        shirt   colander   blouse   strainer

9. Choose the correct homophone.

        Look over (they're / their / there)!

10. Underline the common nouns.

    Mr. Richmond showed Angie a clarinet, a trumpet, and two flutes.

11. Draw a line between the subject and predicate in the sentence above.

12. Remember, the pronouns *he, she*, and *it* are used with the word *has* to
    make contractions. Write the contractions.

    he has ➜ _____

    she has ➜ _____

    it has ➜ _____

Lesson #101

1. **Interjections are words like *ouch*, *hey*, *oh my*, and *wow*. They show strong feeling.** Sentences with interjections often end in an exclamation mark and may be part of a quote. Underline the interjections.

   "Hey, look at that crowd!" yelled Tim. "Wow!" answered Karen.

2. Make nouns by adding the suffix *–sion* to these verbs. extend depress
   Use a dictionary to check your work.

   _____　　　_____

3. Rational means "able to think clearly." What does *irrational* mean?

   _____

4. What is the root of these words?

   suitable unsuitable suited unsuited　　_____

5. Use a comma before a conjunction that separates two independent clauses.
   Example: Ketzia was late for school, but she did not receive a
   　　　　　　detention.
   Underline the conjunction in the example above.

6. Choose the best word to complete the sentence.

   Abigail had to choose (between / among) finishing her homework
   and practicing piano.

7.   Fill in a word to complete the analogy.

Dallas : United States :: Paris : _____

Italy   France   city

8 – 12.   Read the prompt and use this graphic organizer to help you complete the first step of **The Writing Process** (prewriting).

Imagine that you have been put in charge of organizing a playroom for an after school program. You can equip the room with any educational or entertainment items that you want.

In the first column list the things you will need. List details about each item in the second column.

Items	Details about each item

Lesson #102

1. Write the contraction.

    it had → _____

2. If a word ends in a consonant + a silent –e drop the –e when adding a
    suffix that begins with a vowel or –y.
    Example: late → later, noise → noisy
    Add the suffix –ing to the words *excite* and *love*.

    _____   _____

3. **The opposite of** *friend* **is** foe. Underline another word for *foe*.

    police   pal   enemy   stranger

4. Each month of the year has an abbreviation. The abbreviations begin
    with a capital letter and end in a period. Write the correct abbreviation
    next to its full name.   Jan.   Nov.   Apr.   Aug.   Oct.

    November _____   August_____   January _____

5. Write the abbreviations for *Thursday*, *Saturday*, and *Sunday*.

    _____   _____   _____

6. Add quotation marks.

    What happened? exclaimed Mother. Luke answered, We're

    making breakfast!

7. **An interjection can stand alone with an exclamation point.**
   Example: Wow! Aha! Oops! A comma comes after the interjection if
   it is part of a sentence. Ouch, that pan is hot!
   Insert a comma and exclamation point.

   Oops now I've dropped it

8. Underline the cause.

   The pan was so hot Nina dropped it on the floor.

Use a dictionary or thesaurus to find the meaning of each underlined word.

9. Despite change of habitat, coyotes manage to <u>subsist</u> over most of
   North America.

   _____

10. Ranchers are not fond of coyotes because they attack sheep and
    cattle, but farmers may also have an <u>aversion</u> to coyotes.

    _____

11. Although the animal is known as a predator, hungry coyotes have
    been known to <u>plunder</u> watermelon crops.

    _____

12. Write the misspelled word correctly.

    The coyote is a beautyful animal with yellow striking eyes, a bushy
    tail, and pointed ears.

    _____

Lesson #103

1. Something that is *valid* is true. What is the meaning of *invalid*?

    _____

2. What is the root of these words? action   inaction   acting   acted

    _____

3. Underline the conjunction that joins two phrases in this sentence.

    I hope lots of candy and some little toys will be in my basket.

4. Choose a synonym for the underlined word.

    My mother was <u>furious</u> when I didn't come home on time!

    angry   happy   bothered   sleepy

5. Write an abbreviation next to each month.

    Feb.   Mar.   Apr.   Aug.   Sept.   Oct.   Nov.

    February _____ September _____ March _____

6. The word *wind* could be 1) a verb that means "to coil up" or 2) a noun that means "blowing air." Which meaning goes with each sentence?

    The coldest <u>wind</u> blows from the north. _____

    Don't forget to <u>wind</u> your alarm clock and set it. _____

7. Draw a line between the subject and the predicate.

    Coyotes are very clever.

8. Rewrite these as one sentence with a compound predicate.

   Coyotes eat almost anything. Coyotes are very adaptable.

   _____

9. Fill in the missing past tense verbs.

   get / got / _____   choose / _____ / chosen

10. Use an exclamation point if the interjection stands alone; use a comma after the interjection if it is part of a sentence.
    Insert the correct punctuation after each interjection.

    Good grief Where did I put my glasses? Whew here they are.

11. Words containing *mini* mean "small." Use what you know to match these words with their meanings.

    minibus   a small bus

    minimum   to make smaller

    minify   the smallest amount possible

12. Write the sentence correctly.

    Coyotes they sing together in a pack, and They communicate with

    almost a dozen different sounds ⊙

    _____

    _____

Lesson #104

1. Eva knew that <u>she'd</u> been the best flute player. Write the words that were used to form the contraction.

   _____ _____

2. If a word ends in a consonant + –y change the –y to i when adding a suffix. **Example:** happy + -ness ➔ happiness

   beauty + -ful ➔ _____

3. Choose a synonym for the underlined word.

   When the bell rang everyone left and the playground was <u>vacant</u>.

   busy   crowded   noisy   empty

4. Write each abbreviation next to its full name.

   Jan.   Feb.   Mar.   Sept.   Oct.   Nov.   Dec.

   October _____   April _____   December _____

5. You may have used a *comb* to "rake through" your hair. The verb *comb* also means "to search." What is a *beachcomber*?

   a hairdresser   a type of yard tool

   someone who looks for
   things on the beach   all of these

6. A _____ names a person, place, or thing.

7. **Use the pronoun *I* in the <u>subject</u> of your sentence; use the pronoun *me* in the <u>predicate</u>.** Choose the correct word to complete the predicate of this sentence.

    The teacher called on Scott and (I / me) to read aloud.

8. Insert the correct punctuation after each interjection.

    Hurray our team won!   Wow that was close!

9. Underline two adverbs in this sentence.

    You want to completely soak the sponge and wipe lightly.

10. Choose the correct past tense verb.

    Tyler (fall / fell / fallen) from the top of his bunk bed.

11. Use two editing marks to correct this sentence.

    wearing a bicycle helmet is one of
    the smartest things you can do

12. Rewrite the sentence correctly.

    _____

    _____

Lesson #105

1. Write a contraction for *you have*.

   _____

2. If a word ends in a consonant + –*y* change the –*y* to *i* when adding a
   suffix. **Example:** merry + -ment ➔ merriment

   study + -ed ➔ _____

3. What is the root of these words?

   dislike   likely   likeable   likeness

   _____

4. Underline the conjunction that joins two phrases in this sentence.

   Meet me at the bus stop or at the corner.

5. Choose a synonym for the underlined word.

   The mother horse stayed close to its <u>foal</u>.

   baby horse   cowboy   trainer   calf

6. Fill in a word to complete the analogy.

   garbage : trash :: shut : _____

   open   close   door

7. Choose the correct homophone.

   Each person paid (to / too / two) dollars for a ticket.

8. **Prewriting, drafting, revising, editing**, and **publishing** are the five steps of **The Writing Process**. In which step do you choose and explore a topic?

   —————————————

9. **A *fact* is a statement that can be proven. An *opinion* states a personal view or belief.** Which of these is a fact?

   No one should be allowed to ride a bike without a helmet.

   Wearing a bicycle helmet greatly reduces the rider's risk of head injury.

10. Look at the pronouns *I* and *me*. Are they in the <u>subject</u> or the <u>predicate</u>? Circle the pronoun that is correct in each sentence.

    (I / me) played hide and seek with the children.

    Louis found my brother and (I / me) right away.

11. Negatives are words like *no, none, nobody, nothing, never*, and all of the "not contractions." **Do not use two negatives in the same sentence.**
    Example: Incorrect: Nobody tells me nothing!
                Correct: Nobody tells me anything!
    Rewrite this sentence correctly.

    Jason didn't bring no lunch today.

    —————————————————————————

12. Rewrite this sentence without the double negative.

    I don't never forget about eating!

    —————————————————————————

Lesson #106

1. Write a contraction for *I had*.

    _____

2. Use the suffix *–ful* to write a word that means "full of waste."

    _____

3. If a word ends in a consonant + *–y* change the *–y* to *i* when adding a suffix. **Example**: beauty + -ful ➔ beautiful

    plenty + -ful ➔ _____

4. Children <u>yearn</u> for summer vacation in the springtime. To *yearn* means "to _____."

    despise   long for   forget   climb

5. Choose a synonym for the underlined word.

    My baby brother lets out a <u>wail</u> when he feels hungry.

    giggle   large fish   loud cry   soft sound

6. Another word for "written work" is *copy*. What do you think a *copywriter's* job is?

    drawing   reading   writing   singing

7. Underline the possessive pronoun.

    He gave his chair to her.

8 – 12. Read the prompt and write a draft of at least five sentences. Imagine that you could take three people with you on a trip around the world. Who would you take and why?

_____

_____

_____

_____

_____

_____

_____

Lesson #107

1. Write a contraction for *I have*.

    _____

2. Use the suffix *–ful* to write a word that names a type of thinking that is "full of wishing."

    _____

3. What is the root of these words?

    prejudge   misjudge   judgment

    _____

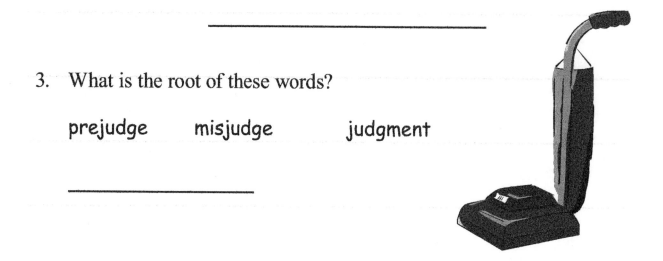

4. Underline the conjunction that joins two phrases in this sentence.

    Shauna washed the windows and ran the sweeper.

5. Which is a synonym for the underlined word?

    The heavy sunflower is held up by a <u>rigid</u> stem.

    stiff   colorful   easy   flexible

6. A _____ names a person, place, or thing.

    verb   noun   pronoun

7. **A *fact* is a statement that can be proven. An *opinion* states a personal view or belief.** Underline the sentence that states an opinion.

    Louise is absent from school today. Louise misses entirely too much school.

8. Rewrite this sentence so that it makes sense.

    Ginny never wears no shoes in the summertime.

    _____

9. Remember, irregular verbs do not end in –*ed*. Write the past tense forms of the irregular verb *come*.

    come, _____, have / has / had _____

10. Choose the correct homophone.

    (Would / Wood) you like to

    come with me to the fair?

11. Underline the subject. Write the verb.

    The sailor was on deck.   _____

12. Proper nouns always begin with a _____ letter.

Lesson #108

1 – 4. You have learned all eight parts of speech. Read the paragraph and look at the underlined words. Decide each underlined word's part of speech and list it in the proper place below. (The eight parts of speech are **noun, pronoun, verb, adjective, adverb, conjunction, preposition,** and **interjection.**)

Hey, do you like to use tools to build things? Are you good at math? If so, you may want to think about a career as a carpenter. Carpenters build things like cabinets and even houses out of wood and other materials. They have to be good planners and clever problem solvers. Carpenters need to be fit and flexible because their work involves bending, kneeling, and carrying heavy loads. They climb up and down ladders. Carpenters work patiently even in rough weather.

Hey - _____   you - _____   build - _____

cabinets - _____   clever - _____   and - _____

down - _____   patiently - _____

5. Write a contraction for *you had.*   _____

6. The prefix *mis–* means "badly" or "wrongly." What is the meaning of *misuse?*

_____

7. Underline two adjectives.

Penny rode the yellow bus to the old schoolhouse.

8. **A *fact* is a statement that can be proven. An *opinion* states a
    personal view or belief.** Which of these is a fact?

    Carpenters are the hardest working people.

    Carpenters use math skills in their daily work.

9. Timothy is such a joker. He's always playing
    <u>pranks</u>. What are *pranks*?

    music   tricks   cards   sports

10. Are you somewhat *agile* or somewhat *awkward*? Circle the word that
    you think describes you, and then find the word in a dictionary. Write
    the meaning of the word you chose.

                    agile   awkward

    _____

11. Choose the correct homophone. Use a dictionary to check the spelling.

                (Write / Right) your name neatly.

12. Rewrite these as one sentence with a compound subject.

    Timothy never gets into trouble because he makes people laugh.
    Ryan never gets into trouble. He also makes people laugh.

    _____

    _____

    _____

Lesson #109

1. Write a contraction for *they have*.

   _____

2. Fill in a word to complete the analogy.

   round : basketball :: _____ : cotton

   soft   clothes   candy

3. Use the prefix *dis–* to write a word that is the opposite of the word *agree*.

   _____

4. Choose a synonym for the underlined word.

   The <u>infant</u> was just learning to crawl.

   sister   boy   baby   puppy

5. Are you feeling *perturbed* or *serene*? Circle one and then look up the word in a dictionary. Write the meaning of the word you chose here.

   perturbed   serene

   _____

6. Write the plural of *country*.

   _____

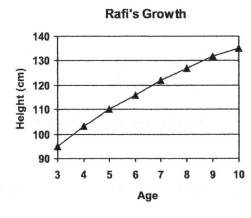

Graphs, charts, tables, and diagrams show information visually. You can understand and use the data quickly if you know how to read these visual displays. Rafi's parents kept a record of his growth by measuring Rafi's height in centimeters. Here is a line graph showing Rafi's growth.

7. What is the title of the graph? _____

8. How old was Rafi when his parents started to record his height? _____

9. Why does the line graph climb higher and farther to the right side of the page?

   A) Rafi is getting older.   C) Both A & B are true.

   B) Rafi is getting taller.

10. If the trend continues, about how tall will Rafi be next year?

          160 cm   125 cm   140 cm

11 – 12. Rewrite these sentences correctly.

Tornadoes can crop up at any time, but in springtime is Tornado Season in the United States. tornadoes are the most violent storms on earth

_____

_____

_____

Lesson #110

1. Replace the underlined words with a contraction.

    Please <u>do not</u> slam the door!   _____

2. Add the suffix *–ed* to change the verb to past tense.

    float _____   paint _____ fix _____

3. Use the prefix *im–* to write a word that means "not proper."

    _____

4. What is the root of these words?

    inequality   unequal   equally   equality   _____

5. Underline the conjunction that joins two phrases in this sentence.

    The boys ordered two kinds of pizza and the loaded potato
    wedges.

6. We have picnics on the <u>patio</u>. A *patio* is most like a _____.

    basement   bedroom   kitchen   porch

7. Choose the correct past tense verb.

    Isabella and Jackie have (get / got / gotten) their new shoes.

8. Use one of the verbs of *being* (is, are, was, were, be, am) in a sentence.

    _____

9. Each state has a two letter postal abbreviation. The letters are always capitalized and are not followed by a period. See if you can match these postal abbreviations with the state's full name.

    OH   KY   PA

    Pennsylvania _____   Ohio _____   Kentucky _____

10. A _____ takes the place of a noun.

11. Rewrite this exclamation correctly. Be sure to insert a comma after the interjection and add the end mark.

    Hey look at those beautiful tulips

    _____

    _____

12. Underline the adverb that compares.

    Now your heart is working harder because you've been running.

Lesson #111

Read this paragraph about a famous Ohioan and use it to complete items 1 – 5.

      Kettering, Ohio was named for an amazing inventor by the name of Charles Franklin Kettering. Charles Kettering invented hundreds of gadgets, including a generator, electrical and mechanical devices for cars, and medical equipment. In addition to being an intelligent creator, Kettering was a teacher, farmer, scientist, and engineer. Charles Kettering also established the Kettering Foundation and the Sloan-Kettering Cancer Center. He was a brilliant and generous man.

Facts taken from http://encyclopedia.thefreedictionary.com.

1. Underline the sentence that states an opinion.

2. List four adjectives used to describe Charles Kettering.

    _____ _____

    _____ _____

3. What is the tense of the verbs in this paragraph?

             past   present   future

4. Underline a subject pronoun.

5. Underline proper nouns that name a city and state.

6. Write a contraction for *he had*.   _____

7. Write a word that ends in *–ment* and is a synonym for *quarrel*.

The boys had an _____ about who would be first.

8. The word *literate* means "able to read and write." What is the meaning of the word *illiterate*?

    _____

9. Choose a synonym for the underlined word.

    The <u>goslings</u> followed the mother goose.

    baby geese   hunters   insects   children

10. Use the editing mark for "take out something" to fix the double negative.

    I didn't never get a chance to work at the computer.

11. Rewrite the sentence correctly.

    _____

    _____

12. Write another sentence using a negative correctly. (none, no, never, nothing, nobody, not, etc.)

    _____

    _____

Lesson #112

1. Replace the underlined words with a contraction.

   <u>It has</u> been a week since I started piano lessons.

   _____

2. Which two words mean almost the same?

   immoral   uneducated   illiterate   mismatch

3. Write a word that means "full of waste."   _____

4. What is the root of these words?

   producer   production   produced   _____

5. Underline the conjunction that joins two phrases in this sentence.

   You can start your homework now and finish later.

6. Denzel loves to travel up the river in a <u>kayak</u>.
   A *kayak* is a type of _____.

   bicycle   car   train   canoe

7. The prefix *fore–* means "before or earlier."
   Example: The typewriter was a <u>forerunner</u> of the modern word
         processor.
   What is the meaning of the underlined word?

   something that came after   something that came before

   something that is used for writing   someone who runs four laps

8. Which sentence is written correctly?

We're moving, so I won't be going to that school no more.

Nobody ever remembers to put out the trash.

9. Rewrite the incorrect sentence from the item above, so that it makes sense.

_____

_____

Another kind of graph is a pie graph. A pie graph shows how something is divided into parts. This graph shows how much of each nutrient is found in a walnut. Look at the graph and use it to answer the last three questions.

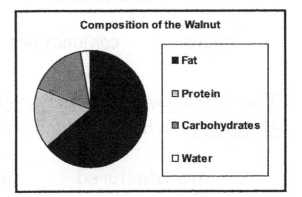

10. According to the pie graph, walnuts are mostly _____.

water   carbohydrates   fat

11. About what percentage of the walnut is water?

2.8%   63.8%   16.9%   16.5%

12. Which two nutrients are about equal in the walnut?

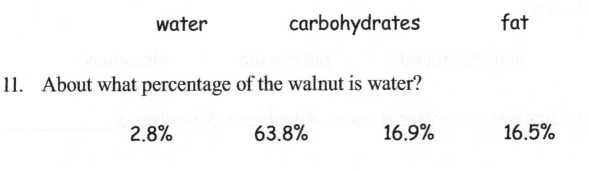

Lesson #113

1. Fill in a word to complete the analogy.

   apple : fruit :: hammer : _____

   board   nail   tool

2. Use the prefix *in–* to write a word that means "the opposite of *direct*."

   _____

3. under, through, about, inside, over, up without, around, near, into
   This is a list of _____.

   nouns   conjunctions   prepositions   verbs

4. The clothing was <u>manufactured</u> in Taiwan but was <u>purchased</u> <u>elsewhere</u>. Which of the underlined words means "in another place"?

   manufactured   purchased   elsewhere

5. Which of the underlined words in item 4 refers to items that are made in a factory?

   manufactured   purchased   elsewhere

6. An adjective describes a noun. An adverb describes a _____.

7. Underline the comparative adverb.

   My kite flies higher than the trees!

8. Here is a set of directions for feeding a dog. See if you can put the steps in the proper order. Number the steps from 1 - 5.

_____ Next, get the gravy from the refrigerator and shake it well.

_____ Finally, put Fido's dish on the floor and call him so he will eat.

_____ Then, measure two tablespoons of gravy and stir it into the dog food.

_____ Put two heaping scoops of dog food into the dish.

_____ First, get Fido's dish and food out of the cupboard.

9 – 10. Use two editing marks to correct each of the sentences.

Although recycling Newspaper takes very little effort, it very important.

did you no that recycling paper can save hundreds of trees every year?

11 – 12. Rewrite both sentences correctly.

_____

_____

_____

_____

Lesson #114

1. Which of these is a contraction? Which is a possessive?

    its   it's   it is

    contraction - _____ possessive - _____

2. Add the suffix *–ful* to make a word that means "full of use."

    _____

3. The word *mobile* means "movable." What does *immobile* mean?

    _____

4. Underline the conjunction that joins two phrases in this sentence.

    Doris wore her white dress and put ribbons in her hair.

5. The root *form* means "shape," *uni* means "one," and *trans* means "change." Match these words with their meanings.

    format   always the same shape

    uniform   size and shape

    transform   change the shape

6. Underline the common nouns in this list.

    Jupiter   comets   satellites   Venus   scientists   Copernicus

7. Fill in a possessive pronoun that agrees with the subject.

    Mike traded _____ baseball cards for some gum.

Read the directions.

> Get some milk out of the refrigerator and fill a glass almost full. Be sure to put the container of milk back in the refrigerator. Next, get the chocolate syrup and shake it well. Then, pour the syrup into the glass of milk. Stir it with a spoon until the syrup is dissolved. Enjoy your chocolate milk!

8. What is missing from the directions?

   A) The directions do not tell how long to stir the milk.
   B) The directions do not tell how much syrup to add to the milk.
   C) The directions do not tell how much milk to use.
   D) Nothing is missing from the directions.

Read this paragraph and use it to complete items 9 – 11.

> Our solar system is made up of the sun planets comets meteors and asteroids. Scientists, called astronomers, have studied these **celestial bodies** for centuries. It is fascinating to look at the sky through a telescope! By studying the solar system, astronomers learn about the world.

9. The first sentence is missing some commas. Insert the commas where they are needed.

10. Underline the sentence that states an opinion.

11. What is the meaning of the words *celestial bodies*?

   objects in space   people who study space
   clouds and angels   none of these

12. Insert editing marks for "take something out," "lower case," and "end punctuation" to correct this sentence.

   Edmond Halley he was an Astronomer who studied comets

Lesson #115

1. Replace the underlined words with a contraction.

   Sabrina <u>should not</u> cross the street alone. _____

2. Add one of these suffixes to the word *friend*. Write the word.

   -y   -ness   -ly   _____

3. What is the root of these words?

   incomplete   completely   completion   _____

4. Underline the conjunction that connects two words in this sentence.

   Would you like ham or chicken on your sandwich?

5. Earthquakes are unpredictable. No one can <u>foresee</u> when or
   where they will happen. What is the meaning of the underlined word?

   to know about a thing before it happens   to be able to see a long distance

   someone who studies earthquakes   all of these

6. A prepositional phrase begins with a preposition and ends with a noun
   (or pronoun). Underline the prepositional phrase.

   Marnie was amazed when she first looked through a telescope.

7. Choose the verb that is a form of *be*.

   The sailor was on deck when the captain shouted his name.

Read these sentences.

A) Are you keeping a <u>record</u> of your weekly quiz scores?

B) The teacher will <u>record</u> our scores after we check our work.

8.   In which sentence is *record* a verb that
     means "to write something down"?   _____

9.   In which sentence is *record* a noun that means "a list"?   _____

Study the chart and use it to answer the next three questions.

Endangered Species			
Animal	Snow Leopard	Atlantic Salmon	Rhinoceros
Habitat	mountains	oceans	open range
Location	Asia	Europe & North America	Africa & Asia
Group	mammal	fish	mammal

10.   Which animal is not a mammal?   _____

11.   Which animal does not live on land?   _____

12.   Which animal can be found in Asia but not in Africa?

      _____

Lesson #116

1. Write a contraction for *she had*.   _____

2. Which two words are synonyms?

   impatient   unmovable   immobile   uncomfortable

3. Underline the conjunction that joins words in this sentence.

   The flag is red and green.

4. *uni – one, bi – two* Why would it be more difficult to balance yourself on a *unicycle* than on a *bicycle*?

   A unicycle _____.

   is bigger   has one wheel   has two pedals

5. What is the root of these words?

   friendless   friendly   unfriendly   friendship

   _____

6. Underline the prepositional phrase.

   There may be skunks living under our porch.

7. Add quotation marks and an end mark.

   Ouch   You stepped on my foot.

Look at this diagram of a cell. Use the diagram to answer questions 8 - 10.

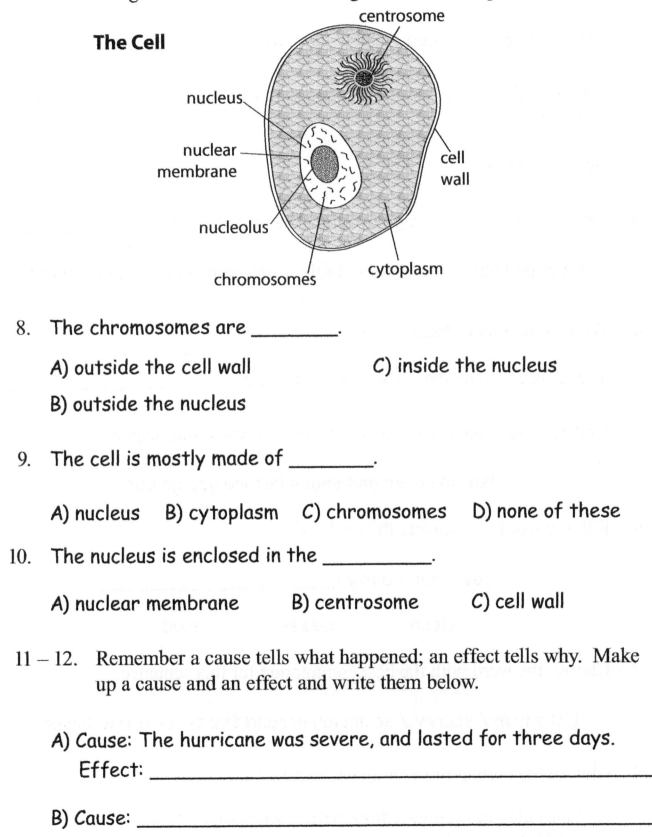

8. The chromosomes are _____.

    A) outside the cell wall   C) inside the nucleus

    B) outside the nucleus

9. The cell is mostly made of _____.

    A) nucleus   B) cytoplasm   C) chromosomes   D) none of these

10. The nucleus is enclosed in the _____.

    A) nuclear membrane   B) centrosome   C) cell wall

11 – 12. Remember a cause tells what happened; an effect tells why. Make
          up a cause and an effect and write them below.

    A) Cause: The hurricane was severe, and lasted for three days.
       Effect: _____

    B) Cause: _____
       Effect: Everyone got a free ticket to the next movie.

Lesson #117

1. Replace the underlined words with a contraction.

    Baji says <u>she has</u> been to New York before.   _____

2. Add one of these suffixes to the root word *confuse*. Spell the new word correctly.

    -ion   -ness   -est   _____

3. The bicycle chain is <u>irremovable</u>. The underlined word means _____.

    not repairable   not redeemable   not removable   all of these

4. What is the root of these words?

    undecided   decision   decisive   decided   _____

5. Underline the conjunction that joins two words in this sentence.

    Put on socks and shoes before you go out.

6. Fill in a word to complete the analogy.

    buy : sell :: dirty :_____

    clean   messy   mud

7. Choose the word with the best connotation for this sentence.

    Let's (run / scurry / scamper) around the track a few times.

8. Choose the correct pronoun in each sentence.

    (I / me) played hide and seek with my cousins. Louis found (I / me) right away.

9. **A simile is a way to describe something by using a comparison.** A
    simile compares two things using the words *like* or *as*.
    Example: In the morning <u>my baby sister</u> is as playful as a <u>kitten</u>.
    (My baby sister is being compared to a kitten.)
    Underline the two things being compared in this simile.

    The workers were as busy as bees this afternoon.

10. Rewrite these as a single sentence with a compound predicate.

    Dolores visited the science museum. She shopped at the
    museum store.

    _____

    _____

11. Write the plural of these nouns: ox   sheep   duck   fox

    _____   _____   _____   _____

12. This sentence has been edited. Write it correctly below.

    Today johnny will graduate from kindergaren. *sp*

    _____

    _____

    _____

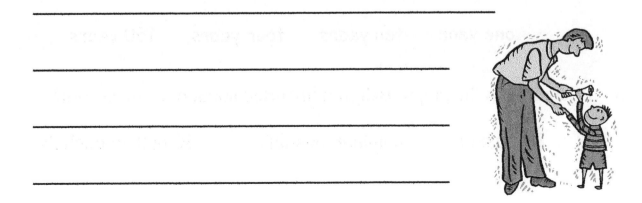

Lesson #118

1. Replace the underlined words with a contraction.

   Carlos is hurrying because <u>he is</u> late.   _____

2. Add one of these suffixes to the root word *pretty*. Spell the new word correctly.

   -ion   -ible   -est   _____

3. Which word means "to send something into the air"?

   launch   lunch   land   lock

Study the bar graph and use it to answer the next three questions.

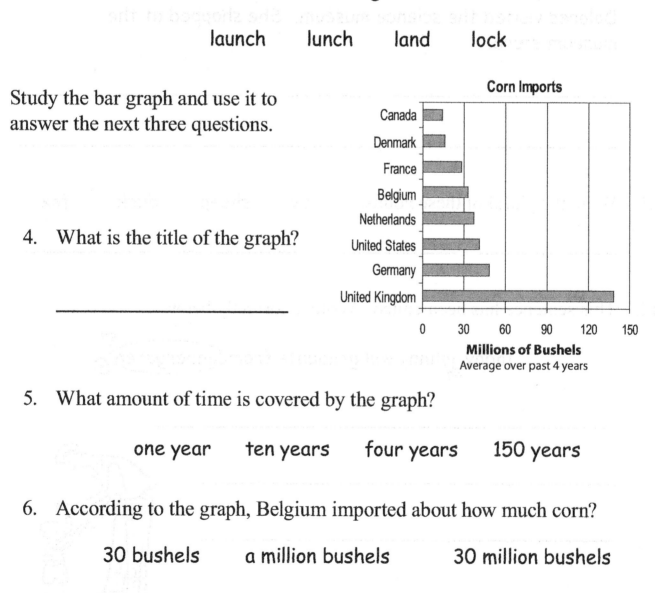

4. What is the title of the graph?

   _____

5. What amount of time is covered by the graph?

   one year   ten years   four years   150 years

6. According to the graph, Belgium imported about how much corn?

   30 bushels   a million bushels   30 million bushels

7. All of these words have the same root: navy naval navigate navigable.
    What does the root *nav* mean?

                    ship   place   shape   sun

8. Write these names correctly.   dr vincent   mrs wilder

    _____   _____

9 – 12. Read this passage. Replace each of the underlined words with a
         better word. Find your words in a dictionary or thesaurus.

    It was a hot (_____) summer day when

    Nathan reached into the freezer. He was happy (_____) to

    see that there was one banana flavored icy-pop. When he pulled

    off the wrapper, Nathan was upset (_____).

    The icy-pop was only half there! It looked like the icy-pop maker

    had run out of banana juice in the middle of making this pop, and it

    was small (_____). Nathan thought about what to

    do, and he decided to write a letter of complaint to the

    icy-pop makers.

Lesson #119

1. Replace the underlined words with a contraction.

    The door was jammed so it <u>would not</u> open.   _____

2. Which word means "to judge badly"?

    prejudge   judgment   misjudge

3. Underline the conjunction that joins two independent clauses in this sentence. Insert a comma before the conjunction.

    It is early in December but the ground is covered with snow!

4. I am <u>doubtful</u> that you will pass the test if you do not study.
    What does *doubtful* mean?

    certain   positive   pleased   unsure

5. What do you think a *ghostwriter* is?

    a Halloween costume   an invisible character

    a writer who uses someone else's name

6. Underline the two things being compared in this simile.

    The children were as quiet as falling snow.

7. Underline the conjunction.

    Will you take the bus or walk home today?

8. What is the subject pronoun in the sentence in item 7? _____

9. Use the editing mark for "add something" to insert a past tense verb.

Jacob his toast with butter.

10. Write the abbreviation for April.

_____

11. Jannise shouted with <u>glee</u> when she saw all the gifts.
    A synonym for the underlined word is _____.

    fear   anger   loud   joy

12. Rewrite this sentence correctly.

    Nobody ever listens to nothing I say.

_____

_____

Lesson #120

1.　Write a contraction for *it had*.　　　　　_____

2.　What two things are being compared in this simile?

My room is cold as a freezer!

_____　　　　　_____

3.　Use the prefix *dis–* to write an antonym for *infected*.

_____

4.　If a word has only one syllable or just one vowel sound, double the
   ending consonant when adding a suffix that begins with a vowel.

pop + -er ➜ _____　　　drop + -er ➜ _____

5.　What is the root of the words below?　　　_____

perfectly　　　imperfect　　　perfection　　　imperfectly

6.　Underline the conjunction.　　flat　over　under　so　there

7.　*loom* - a tool or instrument; *heir* - somebody who has the right to receive
   belongings from his elders.
   The jewel box was a beautiful <u>heirloom</u> that was passed down from
   my great grandmother.

What is an *heirloom*?

an older relative　　　a container for gems　　　a valuable item

8. Find the word *example* in a thesaurus. Write a synonym for *example* here.

    _____

9. Write this sentence correctly.

    Many famous physicists were were woman ^sp

    _____

Study the graphs and use them to answer the next 3 questions.

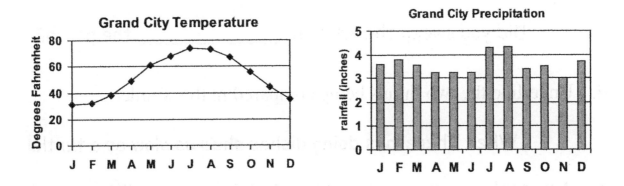

10. These graphs show:

     A) temperatures in Grand City
     B) precipitation in Grand City
     C) both temperature and precipitation

11. What do the letters along the bottom of the graphs stand for?

     _____

12. July and August are the hottest months in Grand City. Which two months are the wettest?

     _____   _____

Lesson #121

1. Which word will you join with *–less* to complete the sentence?

    The gas tank is empty so it is _____ to try to start the car.

    power   point   penny   price

2. Match each prefix with a root word; then write the new words.

    un-   dis-   mis- | spell   equal   appear |

    _____ _____ _____

3. Insert a conjunction.

    Did you sweep the kitchen _____ the porch?

4. Underline the two things being compared in this simile.

    When Theresa is doing dishes she's as slow as a turtle!

5. **A metaphor compares two things but does not use *like* or *as*.** A metaphor uses a form of the verb *be*. **Examples:** If we get into trouble one more time we're toast! We are in a pickle already!

    Underline the metaphor.

    I didn't get enough sleep, and my mind is a blur today.

6. Choose the correct past tense verb.

    Marina has (hide / hid / hidden) my basket in the garden.

7. Choose the correct homophone.

    Look over (they're / their / there)!

8. Write a plural pronoun as the subject of the sentence.

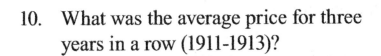 have many flavors of ice cream.

9. Choose the verb that agrees with the subject of this sentence.

    Auntie Emma (go / goes) to church every Wednesday night.

Study the graph below and use it to answer questions 10 – 12.

10. What was the average price for three
    years in a row (1911-1913)?

11. In what year did the lowest average price occur?   _____

12. How much time is covered by this graph?

        10 years   2 years   100 years   1 year

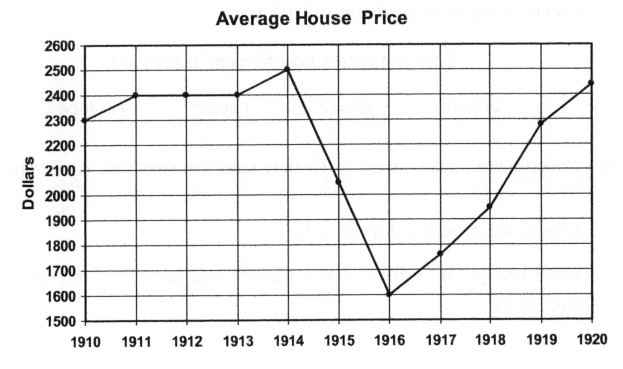

Average House Price

Lesson #122

1. Replace the underlined words with a contraction.

   Sofia wants a blanket because <u>she is</u> cold.   _____

2. Fill in a word to complete the analogy.

   spoke : wheel :: wheel : _____

          bike   turn   ground

3. Write three more words with the ending –*ly*.

          kindly   costly   mostly

   _____   _____   _____

4. Underline the conjunction.

          track   muscles   and   green

5. Choose a synonym for the underlined word.

   KaMicha knows how to <u>mend</u> a torn net.

        broken   woven   repair   replace

6. Underline the metaphor.   Granny says I'm sunshine in a bottle.

7. Choose the correct past tense verb.

   Emily thought we were at home but she was (mistake / mistook / mistaken).

8 – 12. List a set of directions for playing a game or making something.
Write at least five complete sentences.

Topic:
First
Next
Next
Next
Next
Next
Next
Last

Lesson #123

1. Write the words with prefixes.

   not buttoned ➜ _____

   teach again ➜ _____

2. Add the suffix. Write the new word.

   busy + -est ➜ _____

3. What is the root of these words?

   happily   happiness   unhappy   happier   _____

4. Underline the conjunction that joins two words in this sentence.

   Did you pack your lunch and gym bag yet?

5. President George W. Bush was the *namesake* of another United States president. Who was that president?

   Thomas Jefferson   Bill Clinton

   George H. W. Bush   none of these

6. Underline the metaphor.

   During the party our classroom was a blizzard of activity.

7. Add a comma and quotation marks.

   It's a good thing your smoke detector was working said the firefighter.

8.   Read these sentences. Write a *C* in the space if the sentence states a
      cause; write an E if it states an effect.

      _____ Jaiden lit a candle and forgot to blow it out before he went
              to bed.

      _____ A smoky fire burned in Jaiden's bedroom.

9 – 10. Edit these sentences.

It very dangerus to leave a burning
candle unattended.

Don't never ever play with matches

11 – 12. Rewrite the sentences correctly.

_____

_____

_____

_____

_____

Lesson #124

1. Write a contraction for *is not*.   _____

2. Use the prefix *re–* to make words that match the meanings below.
   Example: fill again ➔ refill

   view again ➔ _____   pay again ➔ _____

3. Add *–est* to form adjectives that compare. **Example:** long ➔ longest

   loud ➔ _____   wide ➔ _____

   cold ➔ _____

4. Underline the conjunction that joins two words in this sentence.

   The baked chicken comes with a salad and potatoes.

5. Fill in the missing past tense verbs:

   run - _____   see - _____   do - _____

6. My grandmother's <u>shears</u> are for cutting fabric, so we shouldn't use them for cutting paper. What are *shears*?

   sewing   knives   scissors   needles

7. Underline the metaphor.

   The sun was a brilliant ball of fire that warmed us as we stood on the porch.

Another type of graph is a pictograph or picture graph. It shows information using symbols or pictures. Below is a pictograph showing the number of doctors in each country of a make-believe continent. Study the graph and answer the questions.

Doctors on the Continent of Dribster	
Nomadia	✚✚✚✚✚
Manistan	✚✚✚✚
Karenia	✚✚✚
New Trimburg	✚✚
Orany	✚

✚ = 10 doctors

8. How many countries are there in Dribster? _____

9. Usually, countries with more wealth have more doctors and better medical care. Which country do you think is the wealthiest?

_____

10. Which country do you think is the poorest? _____

11. According to the graph, which statement is true?

A) Karenia has three doctors and a population of 1,000 people.
B) Karenia has thirty doctors.
C) Karenia has three doctors.

12. What information is not given in this graph?

the title of the graph   the population of each country

the name of each country   a key

Lesson #125

1. Write a contraction for *we had*.   _____

2. Add *–ment* to change the verbs into nouns.

   pay_____ - something that is owed

   move_____ - a motion

3. Fill in a word to complete the analogy.

   piglet : pig :: cub : _____

   chicken   cow   bear

4. What is the root of these words?

   uncaring   careless   careful   carefully   _____

5. Underline the conjunction.

   Would you like strawberry or banana?

6. When cars were invented, the horse-drawn carriage quickly
   became an <u>outmoded</u> form of transportation.
   Choose the meaning of the underlined word.

   out-of-date   moving   a vehicle   modern

7. Which of the underlined parts is a simile?   _____

   <u>Neil is a tiger</u> on the football field, and <u>he's fast as a cheetah</u>.
              1   2

8. Copy these common abbreviations for measures.

    oz. = ounce   pt. = pint   qt. = quart   gal. = gallon

    _____   _____   _____   _____

9. **An idiom has a special meaning in a certain language**. It is not a literal meaning. For example, in America we say "Don't beat around the bush!" This statement has nothing to do with beating or bushes. It means something like this: "Don't waste my time!"
    What is the meaning of the underlined idiom?

    You can get that floor clean with a little <u>elbow grease</u>.

    a type of cleaning solution   hard work   a tool for scrubbing

10. Tell the meaning of this idiom in your own words.

    That test was <u>a piece of cake</u>.

    _____

11 – 12. Use editing marks for "capitalization" and "lower case" to edit these sentences.

Imagine what People who don't speak

english think when they hear our idioms!

it must be very confusing to hear things

like, "Stop pulling my leg!"

Lesson #126

1. Look at these words. What does the prefix mean?

    preheat   prerecord   preshrunk

    _____

2. Use *–less* to write a word that means "the opposite of lawful."

    _____

3. Insert a comma and underline the conjunction that joins two independent clauses in this sentence.

    Will you set your alarm or are you sleeping late tomorrow?

4. Choose the correct homophone.

    (They're / Their / There) going hiking tomorrow.

5. Choose the correct past tense verb.

    Ethan and Ryan (begin / began / begun) playing volleyball
    in the fourth grade.

6. One of the possessives in this sentence is incorrect. Cross it out and write it correctly on the line.

    Ninas' sister dropped her mother's cake and it's a mess!

    _____

7. Underline the adverb.

    Lucy carefully glued the cake back together with icing.

8 – 12. Complete this fact-and-opinion graphic organizer about The Food
         Guide Pyramid. First, write your title at the top. Next, read the
         statements below and decide whether each statement is a fact or an
         opinion. Then write each statement on the organizer.

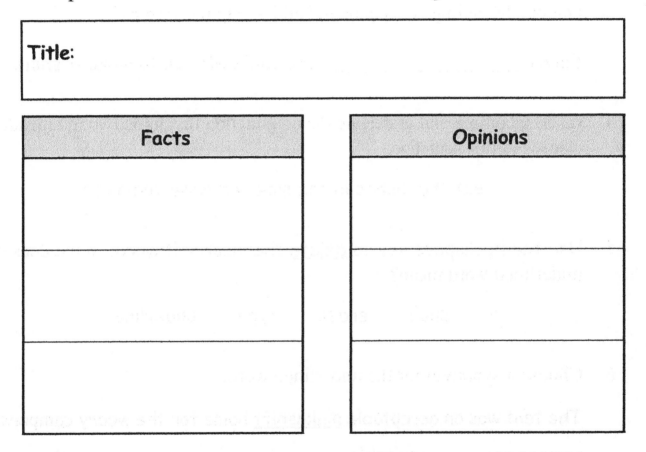

There are five food groups. The Pyramid recommends a wide
variety of foods. Most kids eat too much sugar. Each food group
has recommended daily servings. No one should skip dessert!
Good nutrition doesn't matter if you don't exercise.

Lesson #127

1. Write a contraction for *she has*. _____

2. Place a ✓ next to the prefixes that mean "not."

   _____ un-   _____ im-   _____ pre-
   _____ il-   _____ re-   _____ in-
   _____ mis-   _____ dis-   _____ ir-

3. Double the ending consonant and add *–ed* to the verb *rub*.

   Bernie _____ the table with oil to make it shine.

4. Insert a comma and underline the conjunction that joins two independent clauses in this sentence.

   Put the dishes in the sink and rinse them off.

5. Use the backspace key to <u>delete</u> the incorrect word. What does the underlined word mean?

   spell   erase   type   underline

6. Choose a synonym for the underlined word.

   The tent was an acceptable <u>makeshift</u> home for the weary campers.

   temporary   suitable

   unacceptable   permanent

7. Which of the sentences uses a metaphor?

   That dog is a monster!

   He's as big as a horse!

Read the paragraph before completing items 8 – 12.

Oh no! Here comes that bully, thought Patrick. Patrick had been **taunted** every day by an older boy who rode the bus with him. Patrick knew that fighting on the bus was strictly forbidden but he just couldn't stand it when that bully called him "Pat the Rat." <u>Patrick became a sweltering volcano</u> at the sound of those words. But this time Patrick was ready to just ignore the comments. He had talked with Mrs. Freed, the school counselor. Patrick learned that bullies are looking for a strong reaction, and every time Patrick exploded, the bully was pleased. Patrick had taken an important first step to solving his problem. He had told an adult and asked for help.

8. Write an interjection that you see in the paragraph.   _____

9. What is the meaning of the word *taunted*?

    _____

10. Which two things are being compared in the underlined metaphor?

    _____   _____

11. What was the cause of Patrick's anger?

    A) He had to ride the bus.   B) A bully was calling him names.

         C) Bullies are looking for a strong reaction.

12. When victims get angry or upset, what effect does that have on the bully?

    A) The bully gets angry.   B) The bully stops teasing.

         C) The bully is pleased.

Lesson #128

1. Replace the underlined words with a contraction.

   Leon wants the orange bag because <u>it is</u> bigger.   _____

2. Add the suffixes _–er_ and _–est_ to the word _sweet_. Make two adjectives that compare.

   _____   _____

3. Insert a comma and underline the conjunction that joins two independent clauses in this sentence.

   The movie was great but we ate too much popcorn!

4. Underline all the adjectives in this sentence.

   We had a delicious snack of buttery popcorn and crisp apples.

5. Underline the nouns that should be capitalized.

   I spoke to natasha and mrs. robinson about the book, cinderella.

Here is part of a recipe for making a healthy snack for two people. Read the directions and answer questions 6 – 8.

   First, wash two sticks of celery. Next, trim off the leafy part. Then, spread peanut butter in the curved part of each stick of celery. Finally, sprinkle a few raisins or walnuts over the top of the peanut butter and share with a friend.

6. What are all the ingredients needed for this recipe? List them here.

_____

7. How many servings can this recipe make?

      one   two   three   information not given

8. How many steps are there in the directions?

                _____

9 – 12. Think of a snack that you like to eat or that you have made. Write a recipe for your snack here. Be sure to write clear directions.

_____

_____

_____

_____

_____

_____

_____

_____

Lesson #129

Read the paragraph and use it to answer the first five questions.

What would you do if you knew a friend was cheating? There are many forms of cheating both in and out of school. Ignoring the rules in a game is cheating. Nobody likes to play with a cheater. Having a "cheat sheet" during a test, using a calculator (when you are not supposed to), or lying about information are all forms of cheating. If you copy words directly from another person, this is called plagiarism. Plagiarism is a serious form of cheating with serious consequences. Plagiarism is both illegal and against school rules, because plagiarism is a form of stealing.

1. Is the underlined sentence a fact or an opinion? _____

2. What is plagiarism?

    A) copying another person's work
    B) cheating
    C) a form of stealing
    D) all of these

Read each statement and write T if it is true. Write F if the statement is false.

3. _____ It is okay to do your math with a calculator if your teacher has given permission to do so.

4. _____ If you have done your homework it is okay to let a friend copy it.

5. _____ Using someone else's words without his permission is illegal.

6. Fill in a word to complete the analogy.

raise : lift :: auto : _____

car   bike   tire

7. Combine these sentences. Write one sentence with a compound predicate.

Mom is going to the grocery store. Mom is having lunch with Aunt Marie.

_____

_____

8. Find the word *salve* in the dictionary and look at its meaning and pronunciation. Which letter is silent in the word *salve*?

l   e   both l and e   no letters are silent

9. What is a *salve*?

a type of medicine   a rescue   a type of sale

10 – 12. Write some similes of your own. Complete each of the following.

angry as _____

quick like _____

pretty as _____

Lesson #130

1. Match these prefixes with their meanings.   *re- dis- pre- mis-*

   not - _____ again - _____

   badly - _____ before - _____

2. Add the suffixes *–er* and *–est* to the word *fast* to make adjectives that compare.

   A rabbit runs _____ than a turtle but a

   cheetah is the _____ animal of all.

3. Insert a comma and underline the conjunction that joins two independent clauses in this sentence.

   My dog can do tricks and she is just plain adorable!

4. A desert is a place where water is <u>scarce</u>. What does *scarce* mean?

   dry   plentiful   limited   hot

5. Choose the correct homophone.

   Do you know (whether / weather) or not your mom is at home?

6. Choose the correct past tense verb.

   Olivia and Michael (was / were / been) late for soccer practice.

7. Choose the correct homophone.

   Don't forget to (where / wear) your team tee-shirt!

Read the schedule for the Daily Rapid Transport and answer the questions below.

Daily Rapid Transport ---Tremont to Treeville						
Bus Stop →		Tremont	Campbell	Newberry	Portage	Treeville
Bus Number	1	10:39	10:49	11:13	11:24	11:37
	2	---	10:55	11:19	11:30	11:44
	3	10:51	11:01	11:25	11:36	11:49
	4	---	11:31	11:42	11:56	**12:11**
	5	11:19	11:43	11:54	**12:08**	**12:23**

Bold times denote PM hours.

8. Can a passenger board the Transport in Campbell after 10:30 am and arrive in Portage by 11:30 am? ____________

9. Mona boards the Transport in Newberry at 11:42 am. What time does she arrive in Treeville? ____________

10. Derek lives in Tremont and takes flute lessons in Portage. He needs to arrive in Portage by noon. What is the latest time he can board the Transport in Tremont and still arrive in Portage by noon? ____________

11 – 12. Cross out the fragment. Underline the sentence that has no errors.

Next monday is the day of our class field trip. Bring your permission slips in by Friday. No slip no trip!

Lesson #131

Read this paragraph and use it to answer the first three questions.

In order to avoid plagiarism you should never turn in something that you copied from someone else. You may be able to download and print a report off the Internet. But it is illegal to put your name on it and hand it in for credit. You will find information in books, magazines, or encyclopedias that you can use for your project. But you must write the information in your own words; do not copy. Also, you need to give credit to your sources by listing the name of the author whose work you used to write your report or paper.

1. Is it okay to copy part of your friend's homework if you did the rest yourself?   _____

2. Is it okay to copy notes from an encyclopedia, magazine, or book as long as you cite your source (write the author's name, publisher, and date)?   _____

3. Is it okay to print a report from the Internet and put your name on it?   _____

4. Use prefixes that mean "not" to write words with these meanings.

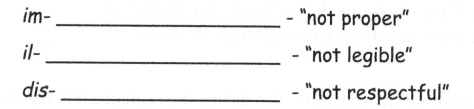

   im- _____ - "not proper"

   il- _____ - "not legible"

   dis- _____ - "not respectful"

5. The marching band <u>incorporated</u> the <u>quickstep</u> into its <u>routine</u>. Look at the underlined words. Which word means "fast footwork"?

   _____

6.   Choose the correct past tense verb.

Hailey had (tear / tore / torn) the page out of her notebook.

7.   I forgot to put on sun screen, and now I'm <u>red as a raspberry</u>!
The underlined phrase is a _____.

simile   metaphor   neither

8.   *Wind* could be 1) a verb that means "to coil up" or 2) a noun that means
"blowing air." Which meaning goes with each sentence?

_____   The coldest wind blows from the north.

_____   Don't forget to wind your alarm clock and set it.

9.   Write this sentence correctly.

Tomorrow it͜Thursday and we will have our
          ∧
          is

music class in the Auditorium.

_____

10 – 12.   Fix this run-on by rewriting it as two or three complete sentences.

Daris is going to do a piano solo at our spring concert Phillip and
Keith will play the trumpet the rest of us will sing.

_____

_____

_____

Lesson #132

1. Fill in a word to complete the analogy.

    Nigeria : Africa :: Canada : _____

    Mexico   North America   United States

2. Add one of these suffixes to the root word *careful*. Spell the new word
    correctly.   -ly   -ing   -est

    _____

3. Underline the conjunction that joins two independent clauses in this
    sentence.

    You should call your brother, or send him an email.

Look at the diagram of a wagon wheel and use it to answer the next three
questions.

4. How many spokes are there?   _____

5. The part in the very center is the _____.

    spoke   axle   hub   none of these

6. What is the wheel of a wagon most like?

    a bicycle tire   a car tire   a truck tire   a ball

7. Choose the correct past tense verb.

    The doctor (be / was / been) very understanding and kind.

8. Choose the correct homophone.

    Marsha isn't going (to / too / two) be in the race today.

9. What are the two things being compared in this simile?

    Mom was mad as a wet hen when she saw the broken dishes.

    _____

10. Read the next sentence and write the meaning of the underlined idiom in your own words.

    The movers knew they were <u>in hot water</u> when Mom showed them the box of dishes.

    _____

11. Edit this sentence.

    the wagon wheel were made it possible for colonists

    to travel and carry their belongings long distances.

12. Rewrite the sentence correctly.

    _____

    _____

    _____

Lesson #133

1. Write a contraction for *they had*.   _____

2. Add one of these suffixes to the root word *subtract*. Spell the new word
    correctly.   *-ion*   *-ness*   *-ful*

    _____

3. What is the root of these words?

    exciting   excitable   unexciting   excitement   _____

4. Underline each independent clause in this sentence.

    Buster misbehaves on the bus, so he is not allowed to ride
    anymore.

5. Which of these words is the opposite of straightforward?

                roundup   roundtable   roundabout

There are eight species of bears. Two of these are the Polar Bear and the Giant
Panda. Study the Venn diagram to see a comparison of these bears, and then
answer questions 6 – 9.

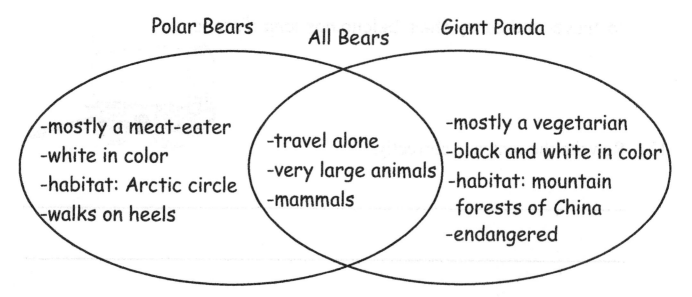

Polar Bears   All Bears   Giant Panda

-mostly a meat-eater
-white in color
-habitat: Arctic circle
-walks on heels

-travel alone
-very large animals
-mammals

-mostly a vegetarian
-black and white in color
-habitat: mountain
   forests of China
-endangered

6. All bears are classified as meat-eaters, but
    they can also eat fruit, nuts, and plant
    leaves. Which bear prefers to eat plants?   _____

7. Which bear is a mammal?   _____

8. Which bear is adapted to a very
    harsh climate where temperatures
    fall well below zero degrees?   _____

9. Underline the statement that is true.

    Bears are solitary (lone).   Bears live and travel in packs.

10 – 12. Use the information in the Venn diagram to write a short report
          about bears. You may want to write a comparison/contrast, telling
          how the two bears are alike and how they are different. Or you may
          decide to focus on just one bear. Write a complete paragraph.

Lesson #134

1. Replace the underlined words with a contraction.

   Louis told me <u>he has</u> known Jake for a long time. _____

2. Underline the word that means "use badly."

   misuse   reuse   useless   useful

3. Underline each independent clause in this sentence.

   Dorothy was disappointed, and she didn't know what to do.

4. What is the conjunction that joins two phrases in the sentence above?

   _____

5. What is the root of these words?

   movable   moving   mover   immovable   _____

6. Choose two synonyms.

   landscape   home   underwater   dwelling

7. The tailor was poor and worked long hours for a <u>meager</u> salary.
   Another word for *meager* is _____.

   plentiful   unfortunate   payment   small

8. What does the underlined idiom mean? Linda studied for the test,
   but she only passed <u>by the skin of her teeth</u>.

   _____

Read the following paragraph. Use the paragraph and what you already know to answer **Yes** or **No** to each of the last four questions.

Most young people know that cheating and plagiarism are wrong, but they may still feel tempted to cheat at one time or another. Students may think that they can not pass a test without cheating. Or they may not know how to write a report in their own words. Kids may think they do not have time or may be too tired to study or work on a report. However, even if it seems like cheating would be an easy way out, even if it seems like it would be okay just one time, cheating is not the answer. It is never acceptable to cheat or plagiarize.

9. Is it okay to sign someone else's
    name to any type of document?   _____

10. Is it okay to let a friend or other person
    copy your work and hand it in for credit?   _____

11. When you write a report, are you supposed
    to tell where you got your facts?   _____

12. Is it okay to look at someone else's work
    just to get ideas for your writing?   _____

Lesson #135

1. List five prefixes that mean "not."

    _____

2. Add one of these suffixes to the root word *hope*. Spell the new word
    correctly.   *-ing*   *-ness*   *-est*

    _____

3. What is the root of these words?

    limitless   unlimited   limited   limiting   _____

4. Underline each independent clause in this sentence.

    I want to ride that roller coaster, but I'm not big enough.

5. Fill in a word to complete the analogy.

    shirt : clothing :: giraffe : _____

    animal   Africa   reptile

6. Underline the conjunction.

    Where are your mittens and scarves?

7. Choose the correct past tense verb.

    Tyler (begun / began / done) his math homework.

8 – 12. Think about these questions and write a draft of at least five
         sentences.

What would you do if you saw a friend cheating? Would you tell an
adult? Would you say something to your friend to try to stop the
cheating? Write a short paragraph explaining what you would do
and why.

_____

_____

_____

_____

_____

_____

_____

Lesson #136

1. Write a contraction for *it has*.   _____

2. Match one of these prefixes with the word *treat*. Write the word that means "treat badly."   *dis-*   *un-*   *im-*   *mis-*

   _____

3. Insert a comma and a conjunction.

   No one came to the door _____ I walked away from the house.

4. The shipbuilders <u>construct</u> <u>vessels</u> that are <u>seaworthy</u>.
                              A   B   C

   Match each of the underlined words above with its meaning.

   _____ a large watercraft   _____ build   _____ able to sail safely

5. Imagine that you are working on a science report. In order to avoid plagiarism you should _____.

   A) copy from a friend

   B) use a variety of sources and list them after your report

   C) download a science report from the internet

6. Karen and (I / me) like to make popcorn balls.

7. She showed (I / me) how to make caramel corn, too.

Look at the illustration below and use it to answer the next 3 questions.

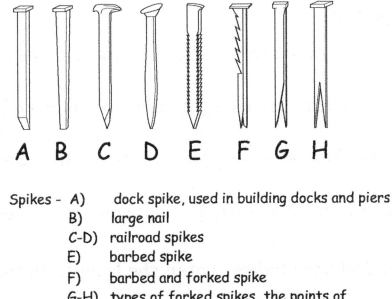

Spikes - A)   dock spike, used in building docks and piers
          B)   large nail
          C-D)   railroad spikes
          E)   barbed spike
          F)   barbed and forked spike
          G-H)   types of forked spikes, the points of
                   which spread and become hooked in
                   the timber when driven.

8. Which spike is barbed but not forked?   _____

9. Which spikes were used to build railroad tracks?   _____

10. Which spikes are forked?   _____

Edit these sentences. Use two editing marks for each sentence.

11. This Summer i plan to join a reading club at my local library.

12. My goal it is to read one or to good books every week.

Lesson #137

Read the paragraph. Below, write the name of each part of speech that is underlined (noun, pronoun, verb, adjective, adverb, conjunction, preposition, interjection).

Hey, have you ever heard of Bessie Coleman? Bessie was the
1.

first African American, female pilot. She lived a brief, but very
                                    2.   3.

courageous, life. Bessie was a gifted student. Although she was
                                  4.

poor and went to school in a meager, one-room schoolhouse,
                         5.

Bessie finished all her studies. Later, she learned to speak
                                                 6.

French so that she could study aviation in France. Bessie was a
               7.

stunt pilot, and she boldly refused to fly in shows that were not
                       8.

open to African Americans.

Facts taken from Women in History, http://www.lkwdpl.org/wihohio/figures.htm

1. _____   5. _____

2. _____   6. _____

3. _____   7. _____

4. _____   8. _____

9. One meaning of the word *finite* is "limited."
What is the meaning of *infinite*?

_____

10. What is the root of these words?

trusting   mistrust   trusted   mistrusted   _____

11. Write the sentence correctly.

Bessie Coleman was a role∧for women and <u>african</u> <u>americans</u>.
                        model

_____

_____

12. Write the sentence correctly.

Today there is a club for (femal)ˢᵖ pilots in

honor of the life of Bessie Coleman ⊙

_____

_____

_____

Lesson #138

1. The pronouns *you, we*, and *they* are combined with the word *are* to make contractions. Write the contractions.

   you are ➔ _____   we are ➔ _____

   they are ➔ _____

2. Write a sentence of your own, using one of the contractions.

   _____

3. Use the prefix *mis–* to write a word that means "handle badly."

   _____

4. Insert a conjunction.

   I really like peanut butter _____ jelly sandwiches!

5. Use a dictionary to determine which word below means "a place where a plant stores its food."

        taproot   uproot   arrowroot

6. Fill in a word to complete the analogy.

   chick : bird :: _____ : sheep

        adult   lamb   wool

Read each of the following lines and decide if the underlined parts are correct.
If there is a mistake, choose the correction below the line. If there is no
mistake, choose "correct as is."

7. <u>Me and Missy</u> have soccer practice every day after school.

   A) Missy and me   B) Missy and I   C) correct as is

8. My mom <u>has took</u> us to all the practices,

   A) has taken   B) have taken   C) correct as is

9. so <u>Missys dad</u> comes to our games.

   A) Missys' dad   B) Missy's dad   C) correct as is

10. <u>Her Dad</u> always says,

    A) Her dad   B) Your dad   C) correct as is

11. "Wow! You girls are <u>real pros!</u>

    A) real Pros!   B) real pros!"   C) correct as is

12. He says that <u>whether</u> we win or lose the game.

    A) weather   B) while   C) correct as is

Lesson #139

1. Underline the meaning of the word *inequality*.

          unending   equal   not equal   even

2. What is the root of these words?

   informal   formally   informally   _____

3. Insert a conjunction.

       I did my homework, _____ I forgot to turn it in.

4. Which sentence shows what *climate* means?

   I prefer a warmer climate.   The climate was not agreeable to me.
   The climate of this region is hot and dry.

5. Select the correct meaning of *climate* in the sentence you chose above.

   A) typical weather in a region   C) sunshine and heat

   B) places you'd like to live   D) the atmosphere

6. Underline the correct past tense verb.

       All the fish have (swim / swam /swum) upstream.

7. Mitzy always <u>gets cold feet</u> right before a piano solo. What does
   the idiom mean?

   A) needs warmer socks   C) becomes fearful or nervous

   B) uses the foot pedals   D) is cold

Write the next two sentences correctly.

8. Nikki and jewel forgot to bring (they're) baseball gloves. *sp*

_____

9. We washed our bikes, and after then we helped my Dad wax his car.

_____

Study this diagram and use it to answer the last 3 questions.

10. Which comes first?

A) first quarter

B) new moon

C) full moon

11. According to the diagram which side of the moon is receiving the light rays of the sun?

A) the white side

B) the shaded side

C) neither of these

12. What is the title of the diagram?

A) The Earth and Moon

B) Sun's Rays

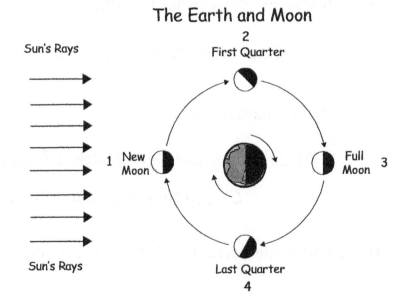

The Earth and Moon

Sun's Rays

2 First Quarter

1 New Moon

Full Moon 3

Last Quarter 4

Sun's Rays

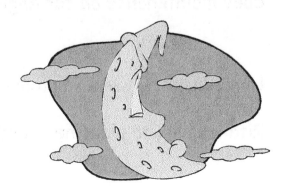

Lesson #140

1. Insert a conjunction.

   Three little pigs _____ a big wolf are the stars of the play.

2. Put your papers in a <u>manila</u> folder and place them in the file drawer. What is *manila*?

   A) a heavy kind of paper   C) a flavor of ice cream

   B) an envelope   D) a filing cabinet

3. Write a contraction for *he has*.   _____

4. Choose the correct homophone.

   Each person paid (to / too / two) dollars for a ticket.

5. What is plagiarism?

   A) studying for a test with a friend   B) using a calculator

        C) putting your name on someone else's work

6. Choose the correct verb form to complete the sentence.

   He (fix / fixes) flat tires and does maintenance on car engines.

7. Underline the possessive pronoun.

   Rita is going to plant her garden today.

8. When you give an oral or written report, are you required to tell where you got your information?

    _____

9. Sandy says your problem is that you worry too much; I think he <u>hit the nail on the head</u> this time. What is the meaning of the idiom?

    A) Sandy is good with a hammer and nails.

    B) What Sandy said was right.

    C) Sandy thinks people shouldn't worry.

10. What is the meaning of all of these prefixes?

    un-   dis-   im-   in-   ir-   il-   _____

11. Write the meaning of each prefix.

    pre- _____   re- _____

    mis- _____

12. Underline the two things being compared in the metaphor. Then write what the metaphor means on the line below.

    The sea became a raging monster at the height of the storm.

    _____

    _____

Minutes a Day-Mastery for a Lifetime!

Level 4

2nd Semester

English Grammar & Writing Mechanics

Help Pages

Help Pages

Vocabulary

Sentence	a group of words that tells a complete thought
Subject	tells *who* or *what* the sentence is about
Predicate	tells what the subject *does* or *is*
Synonym	a word that means the same or almost the same as another word
Antonym	a word that means the opposite of another word

Homophones, homonyms, and homographs are words that sound alike or are spelled alike (or both), but have different meanings. This chart will help you remember which is which.

	Homonyms	Homographs	Homophones
Spelling	same	same	different
Pronunciation	same	different	same
Meaning	different	different	different

Editing Marks

Capital letter	≡
End punctuation	⊙ (!) (?)
Add something	∧
Change to lower case	/
Take something out	℘
Check spelling	ⓢⓟ
Indent	¶

Helping Verbs

is	can	may
are	could	might
am	should	have
was	would	has
were	will	had
	shall	

Help Pages

Parts of Speech

Noun	a word that names a person, place, or thing
Verb	a word that shows action or a state of being; a verb is the main word in the predicate of the sentence
Pronoun	a word that takes the place of a noun
Adjective	a word that describes a noun; an article (*a, an* and *the*) is a special type of adjective
Adverb	a word that describes a verb (often ends in –*ly*)
Conjunction	a word that connects words or phrases in a sentence (*and, or, but, so*)
Preposition	a word that relates a noun or pronoun to other words in a sentence (see list); a <u>prepositional phrase</u> begins with a preposition and ends with a noun or pronoun
Interjection	a word or short phrase that shows emotion Wow! Aha! Oh no!

Prefix	Meaning
un-, dis-, im-, in-, ir-, il-	not
re-	again
mis-	badly
pre-	before

Forms of the Verb *Be*

Present	Past	Future
am	was	will be
is	were	
are		

Kinds of Sentences

Declarative	a statement; tells something	.
Interrogative	a question; asks something	?
Imperative	a command; tells someone to do something	.
Exclamatory	an exclamation; shows emotion	!

Help Pages

Steps in the Writing Process

1. Prewriting	getting ideas for writing
2. Drafting	putting ideas into writing
3. Revising	adding or taking out words to make your writing better
4. Editing	using editing marks to correct mistakes
5. Publishing	sharing your writing with others

Spelling Rules

1. Words ending in *s, x, z, ch,* or *sh,* add *–es* to make the plural.

2. If a word has only one syllable or just one vowel, <u>double the ending consonant</u> before adding *–er* or *–est.*

3. To make compound words, usually join two words without changing the spelling of either word.

4. When adding a suffix to a word, the spelling of the word sometimes changes; the suffix does not usually change.

5. If a word ends in *–e* and you want to add a suffix that begins with a vowel, drop the *–e* before adding the suffix.

6. When a word ends in a consonant plus *y,* change the *y* to *i* and add *–es.*

Rules for Using Quotation Marks

1. Put quotation marks before and after the actual words that someone says. Think of quotation marks as the frame around spoken words. Keep the end mark inside the quotes.
Example: "Here comes Lila!"

2. Use a comma before or after a quote within a sentence.
Examples: Laura exclaimed, "What a beautiful song!"
"Let's get some ice cream," said Jack.

3. Do not use a comma at the end of the quote if there is another punctuation mark.
Example: "Grandma's here!" exclaimed Sasha.

Help Pages

Rules for Using Commas

1. Use commas to separate words or phrases in a series.
   Example: I'll take a dozen eggs, a watermelon, two loaves of bread, and a ham.

2. Use a comma to separate two independent clauses joined by a conjunction. **Example:** He has red hair, and she has gray hair.

3. Use a comma after an introductory word, such as an interjection.
   Example: Hey, where are you going?
   Do not use a comma if there is an end mark after the interjection.
   Example: There it is!

4. Use a comma to separate two words or two numbers, when writing a date. **Example:** Monday, February 20, 2006

Pronouns

Type	Singular	Plural
Subject Pronouns (or Nominative Case Pronouns) are used as the subject of a sentence or clause.	I, you, he, she, it	we, you, they
Object Pronouns (or Objective Case Pronouns) are found in the predicate of a sentence.	me, you, him, her, it	us, you, them
Possessive Pronouns are used to show possession. These possessive pronouns modify a noun.	my, your, his, her, its	our, their, whose
**These possessive pronouns are used alone.	mine, yours, his, hers	ours, theirs, whose

Cause and Effect	An **effect** tells *what* happened. A **cause** tells *why* it happened. (Some clue words for a cause / effect relationship are *because, therefore, so,* and *since*.)
Fact and Opinion	A **fact** can be proven. An **opinion** states a belief or feeling.

Help Pages

Plagiarism	The illegal use of another person's words, putting your name on someone else's work, copying another person's words or work, or not giving credit to a source.
Abbreviation	A shortened form of a word. Some abbreviations, such as social titles, months, and weekdays end in a period. **Examples**: Dr. Mr. Ms. and Mrs. / Sept. Mon. Feb. Thurs. (Postal abbreviations do not end in a period. AK, OH, PA, WV)

Figures of Speech

Simile	a way to describe something by using a comparison; a simile compares two things using the words *like* or *as* **Example**: My sister is *as stubborn as a mule.* (My sister is being compared to a mule.)
Idiom	has a special meaning in a certain language or culture; it is not a literal meaning **Example**: "She is always willing to *go the extra mile.*" This statement has nothing to do with going anywhere. It means someone is a hard-worker or is willing to do extra work.
Metaphor	Compares two things but does not use *like* or *as*; it uses a form of the verb *be* **Example**: He is a tiger on the field! (He is as energetic as a tiger when he is on the field.)

Verb Tenses

Present Tense	Most present tense verbs end in –*s* when the subject is singular. (run ➔ runs)
Past Tense	Verbs that tell an action that has already happened usually add –*ed* to show past time.
Future Tense	Verbs that tell about an action that is going to happen add the helping verb *will* to show future time.

Help Pages

Irregular Verbs

Present	Past	With has, have, or had
am / is / are	was / were	*has, have,* or *had* been
begin	began	*has, have,* or *had* begun
blow	blew	*has, have,* or *had* blown
break	broke	*has, have,* or *had* broken
bring	brought	*has, have,* or *had* brought
choose	chose	*has, have,* or *had* chosen
drive	drove	*has, have,* or *had* driven
fly	flew	*has, have,* or *had* flown
freeze	froze	*has, have,* or *had* frozen
make	made	*has, have,* or *had* made
ring	rang	*has, have,* or *had* rung
say	said	*has, have,* or *had* said
sing	sang	*has, have,* or *had* sung
speak	spoke	*has, have,* or *had* spoken
steal	stole	*has, have,* or *had* stolen
swim	swam	*has, have,* or *had* swum
tear	tore	*has, have,* or *had* torn
tell	told	*has, have,* or *had* told
think	thought	*has, have,* or *had* thought
throw	threw	*has, have,* or *had* thrown
wear	wore	*has, have,* or *had* worn

Some Common Prepositions

about	around	by	in	on	to
above	before	down	inside	out	under
across	behind	during	into	outside	until
after	below	except	near	past	up
along	beside	for	of	through	with
among	between	from	off	throughout	without

Help Pages

Analogy

An **analogy** is a way of comparing things.

Here is an example: mayor : city :: governor : state
This means,

"Mayor is to city as governor is to state."

To solve an analogy, you need to figure out what the relationship is between the two words.

A *mayor* is <u>the leader of</u> a city. A *governor* is <u>the leader of</u> a state.

Here is another example: lamb : sheep :: calf : _____
What is the relationship?   A lamb is <u>a baby</u> sheep.

          horse   piglet   cow   kitten

The missing word must be *cow* because a *calf* is <u>a baby</u> *cow*.

In an **analogy**, the words may be compared in many ways.

The words may be synonyms.

Example: happy : joyful :: tall : high

Happy and *joyful* are <u>synonyms</u>. *Tall* and *high* are <u>synonyms</u>.

The words may be antonyms.

Example: thin : thick :: rich : poor

Thin is the <u>opposite</u> of *thick*. *Rich* is the <u>opposite</u> of *poor*.

One word may describe the other.

Example: bright : sunshine :: prickly : porcupine

Sunshine is *bright*. A *porcupine* is *prickly*.

One word may name a part of the other.

Example: wheels : bicycle :: legs : table

A *bicycle* has *wheels*. A *table* has *legs*.

One word may be in the category or group of the other.

Example: rabbit : mammal :: orange : fruit

A *rabbit* is a type of *mammal*. An *orange* is a type of *fruit*.